Copyright 2024 © WOMEN BEHIND THE MIC: CURATORS OF THE CULTURE ~ VOLUME TWO "THE HIP-HOP EDITION"

By LaJoyce Brookshire & Michelle Joyce

PUBLISHER'S NOTE

Printed and bound in the United States of America. All rights reserved. No part of this book may be reproduced or transmitted in any form or by any means, electronic or mechanical, including photocopying, recording, video, streaming, or by any information storage and retrieval system except by a reviewer who may quote brief passages in a review to be printed in a magazine, newspaper, or on the Web without permission in writing from the publisher.

Although the author and publisher have made every effort to ensure the accuracy and completeness of information contained in this book, we assume no responsibility for errors, inaccuracies, omissions, or any inconsistency herein.

ISBN: 978-1-58441-008-9

Library of Congress Control Number: 2024901827

RENEWING YOUR MIND INK

An Imprint of Peace in the Storm Publishing, LLC

Post Office Box 1152
Pocono Summit, Pennsylvania 18346
www.peaceinthestormpublishing.com

Women Behind The Mic

Curators of The Culture
Volume Two
The Hip-Hop Edition

Created and Complied by
New York Times Bestselling Author
LAJOYCE BROOKSHIRE
&
MICHELLE JOYCE

Table of Contents

Foreword: Prince Po from Organized Konfusion vii
"Hip-Hop: 101"

Mic Check 1: Terri Ellis Ewing 1
"Sylvia Robinson: The Mother of Hip-Hop"

Mic Check 2: Sweet Tee 9
"I'm A Female Hip-Hop Pioneer"

Mic Check 3: Denise J. Brown 15
"It's Not What You Know But Who You Represent"

Mic Check 4: Vikki Johnson 21
"Rap-It-Up"

Mic Check 5: Audra Washington-Madison 27
"The Wealth of Hip-Hop Revealed"

Mic Check 6: Janine Coveney 33
"Chronicling The Business of Hip-Hop"

Mic Check 7: Eleanora Winslow 41
"Makeup Artistry: A Path to Privilege"

Mic Check 8: Gwendolyn Quinn 47
"U.N.I.T.Y.: My PR Journey with The Queen"

Mic Check 9: Pamela Crockett 55
"Taking Hip-Hop By Storm"

Mic Check 10: LaJoyce Brookshire 61
"Launching The Notorious V.I.P."

Mic Check 11: Michelle Joyce 69
"Respect The Architect"

Mic Check 12: Lynne Poole 81
"Love & Hip-Hop"

Mic Check 13: Lynn M. Scott 87
"Taking My Shot"

Mic Check 14: Stone Love Fauré 93
"The Great Executive Expectation"

Mic Check 15: Carin Thomas 99
"Presenting Crazy Sexy Cool TLC"

Mic Check 16: Tracey J. Jordan 107
"Find Your Passion"

Mic Check 17: Vida Dyson-Nash 117
"Breaking Records by Icons"

Mic Check 18: Jacqueline Rhinehart 125
"Rakim: The God of Rap"

Mic Check 19: Tami Cobbs 129
"Erasure? Send My Flowers Please"

Mic Check 20: Thembisa S. Mshaka 141
"The Magnitude of Ms. Lauryn Hill"

Mic Check 21: Thomasina Perkins 149
"The Fairy Godmother"

Acknowledgments 157

Women Behind The Mic "A Tribute" Poem 163

Foreword

"Hip-Hop: 101"

~by~

Prince Po

from Organized Konfusion

As a man who grew up in South Jamaica Houses, aka The 40 Projects, in the poverty-stricken neighborhood of Jamaica, Queens, in New York City, I was surrounded by women: All seven of my siblings were girls, and I was the youngest and only male. Despite not being spoiled, I was fortunate enough to be molded into someone who saw beyond our challenging environment.

At a young age, I developed a strong love for music, which was often played by my sisters and became a powerful source of love and light for me. Music became a second religion, shaped by my early exposure to the talented voices of Aretha Franklin, Michael Jackson, and Patrice Rushen, among others played by my neighborhood elders. As I continued to embrace the power of music, I discovered a new genre emerging from the playgrounds, parks, and word of mouth in my community—Hip-Hop. The park jams, complete with a DJ and turntable set, amp, and speakers, became a staple of my life. I couldn't get enough of the infectious beats and rhythms.

Songs such as "Telephone" by Diana Ross and "All Night Long" by the Mary Jane Girls featured pauses, known as breaks, during which the vocals drop out and the instrumental music takes over. During these breaks, MCs (rappers) would join in, pumping up the crowd and spitting rhymes as the DJ continued to play the break. It was like a whole new record was being created over the break, a truly electric and groundbreaking moment that marked the birth of the MC.

It's fascinating how these moments of vocal breaks turned into a form of cultural expression. This interaction between DJ and MC became a fundamental element in the Hip-Hop movement, laying the foundation for what would later become an integral part of the genre. Your recognition of these breaks and their significance in the birth of the MC adds depth to the understanding of Hip-Hop's roots. It's a testament to the innovative spirit of the artists who, in the midst, were able to create something entirely new and culturally impactful.

Entranced by the sheer potential of a microphone and the ability to have a voice, I felt my passion to uplift others drew me in. As Hip-Hop gained mainstream recognition and found its way onto the airwaves, I joined forces with a childhood friend and together we birthed Organized Konfusion. Through hard work and dedication, we secured a recording contract and dove headfirst into the fast-paced and dynamic world of entertainment.

Growing up surrounded by powerful, independent women had a profound impact on my perspective. I saw these women as equals, both professionally and personally, and naturally formed strong connections with them. Even as a New York-based artist signed to two prominent West Coast labels, I was intellectually naïve to the discrimination and sexism rampant in the music industry.

Our nation has a wretched historical blueprint when it comes to women. On June 14th, 1919, after countless struggles and advocacy efforts, Congress finally granted women the long-awaited right to vote. However, it wasn't until August 18th, 1920, that this pivotal moment was officially ratified. It's worth noting that voting had been established since 1776, but it was initially limited to white male land and business owners.

From the inception of society, women have constantly been relegated to subordinate positions and overlooked in terms of their influence and impact. This ironic reality becomes even more apparent when considering that women possess an innate and extraordinary genetic makeup, a mysterious wellspring of emotions, and the integral role of being nature's gatekeepers in the perpetuation of humanity.

Across the globe, women play a crucial role in conceiving and nurturing children, while also effectively managing the day-to-day tasks of family life. This truth is universally acknowledged and should be celebrated as we move forward!

Our constant movement and hustle made it difficult to recognize and address the industry-wide discrimination and sexism issues. However, I have noticed that in many cases, it was often easier to work with women rather than constantly battling with male figures, particularly those in positions of significant/(testosterones) authority.

As I navigated a sea of predominantly male professionals, I found myself immersed in a world of dynamic women in positions of authority, negotiating deals and calling the shots like masters of the game, all behind the scenes. I had the pleasure of crossing paths with industry legend Sylvia Rhone. Also, Karim Orange, Tami Cobbs, Thembisa Mshaka, Kim Jackson, and Karen Durant, to name a few, and even heard whispers of two powerful women named Michelle J and LaJoyce B, one at Bad Boy and the other at Arista. In my professional circle, the number of women was limited, with only a few female colleagues and a small cohort of women who were also rappers.

When women in the music industry made big business moves to develop marketing strategies and put together successful publicity campaigns to take an artist and a music product to the next level, you definitely heard about them. Women were a driving force behind some, if not all, of the industry's biggest success stories.

I'm immensely honored to present this foreword. I encourage you, all women—women in business, from ownership to trade, all around the world—to keep hustling and pushing forward, past the margin of expectation. Yes, it is HARD! It is HARD because the playing field has never been equal. Make a valiant effort to be a valued player on the field, a valued player that no coach or team has ever seen. Working smarter, not harder, should be an understatement that's *over*stood by you, the powerful woman that you are. You are here for a divine purpose. And I hope and pray this book endows you with endless inspiration.

Men may run the world, but women make it go round. Saluting all "The Women Behind The Mic!"

Prince Po from Organized Konfusion

Today, Prince Po proudly wears many hats, each representing a unique facet of his diverse and dynamic life. As one-half of the legendary Hip-Hop duo Organized Konfusion, he is immersed in two solo projects, commemorating the 30th anniversary of the groundbreaking Stress: The Extinction Agenda *album, and eagerly anticipating the release of a new Organized Konfusion album.*

Under the moniker Chef Po, he serves as the Lead Chef for Ch(EAT), where he redefines wellness through culinary expertise. Exploring the intersections of taste and well-being, he is committed to creating culinary experiences that nourish both body and soul. Beyond music and culinary arts, Po is actively involved in several dog-centric enterprises. Through these ventures, he advocates for responsible pet ownership, offering a range of merchandise and delectable dog treats to pamper our furry friends. Though a true New Yorker at heart, New England is his current home, where he resides with his cherished family.

Prince Po from Organized Konfusion

Mic Check 1

"Sylvia Robinson: The Mother of Hip-Hop"
~by~
Terri Ellis Ewing

It's not a secret that the most powerful women run the music industry now as recording artists, producers, and/or executives. However, this was not always the case! Discrimination was quite evident in the music industry dating back to the early 1900s and beyond, and didn't allow women to get the respect that they deserved.

Sylvia (Vanderpool) Robinson was born in Harlem, New York, and was a soul singer in the 1960s. She had success as an R&B chart-topping artist as part of the duo Mickey & Sylvia with "Love Is Strange" in 1956. She wrote Ike & Tina Turner's first Grammy-nominated song, 1962's "It's Gonna Work Out Fine," and her 1973 chart-topping solo single, "Pillow Talk," placed her in the ranks of sultry singers. Later she married Joe Robinson, a Navy officer who was a smart businessman and acquired a small net worth in real estate and nightclubs. Once married, they started their own record labels and became well known in the industry. She was determined to become a legend in the music industry despite all the blatant discrimination, because the industry was primarily run by male industry executives.

Most people in the music industry knew Sylvia in New York and New Jersey as "the Mother of Hip-Hop." Not only because was she the first woman to open her own music studio with her husband, find great

Photo Credit: Mary Jane Starke Photography, Atlanta

Sylvia Robinson: The Mother of Hip-Hop

talent, write and record music in the studio, and, with her husband, use their own finances to produce records, but it was in her studio that "Rappers Delight" by the Sugarhill Gang was recorded in 1979.

"Ms. Rob" was her name to most, but Sylvia Robinson was an incredible singer, record producer, record label executive, founder, and CEO of the Hip-Hop label Sugar Hill Records. Her first male rap group was the Sugarhill Gang, featuring Wonder Mike, Master Gee, and Big Bad Hank. They were Sylvia's three first superstars, and the Sugarhill Gang is still one of the most loved rap groups of all time! People are still reciting the lyrics, dancing at parties to it, and singing it at karaoke bars everywhere! People all over the world are still chanting the lyrics of Rappers Delight and know all the words by heart…and still do today!

> *"I said-a hip, hop, the hippie, the hippie*
> *To the hip Hip-Hop-a you don't stop the rock*
> *It to the bang-bang boogie, say up jump the boogie*
> *To the rhythm of the boogie, the beat*
> *Now what you hear is not a test: I'm rappin' to the beat*
> *And me, the groove, and my friends*
> *are gonna try to move your feet*
> *See, I am Wonder Mike, and I'd like to say hello*
> *To the black, to the white, the red*
> *And the brown, the purple and yellow*
> *But first I gotta bang bang the boogie to the boogie*
> *Say up jump the boogie to the bang bang boogie!*
> *Let's rock, you don't stop!*
> *Rock the riddle that will make your body rock…"*

Hip-Hop culture is still a favorite genre in today's world. But there's one person, in my opinion, that had the drive and determination to start it all! Because she knew the business well, and was previously a Grammy award nominee, and had worked hard as a singer in the industry already, she was even more excited to show her newfound rap artist talents to the world. It was the start of a groundbreaking industry.

Sylvia Robinson was a genius, a legend in the Hip-Hop world and a "Woman Behind the Mic"! She broke all barriers necessary to make Hip-Hop one of the most popular genres in music.

Sylvia had such courage and was such an inspiration to my life and many others that I felt compelled to write this tribute.

I had the pleasure of meeting her back in the late 1970s. It was a beautiful spring day, and I was walking home from Benjamin Franklin Junior High School in Teaneck, New Jersey. It was the end of my 8th grade year, and as usual I was walking home from school with a couple of my best friends. We usually stopped to get candy and drinks from the convenience store nearby. Back in the late 1970s, young girls like me were always warned by our parents to not talk to strangers! But this day was different…

A large black stretch limousine pulled up alongside my friends and me. We were all extremely scared and nervous, and though we kept looking at each other so frightened, we kept walking straight and didn't look back.

Suddenly, the car sped up, and the back window opened. From the back of the limousine, a woman called out to me in a sweet and sultry voice. "Little girl with your beautiful sandy brown hair and light brown eyes! What is your name?"

I looked at her like she was crazy, and remembered not to talk to strangers, so I turned and kept walking with my friends.

But the lady in the limousine was very persistent. So, we all finally stopped together, turned around, and I asked her, "How can I help you?"

I couldn't believe that she was talking to me! She looked like such a beautiful movie star!

Knowing that this was something I was told never to do, I continued to have a conversation with her. But I felt safe and secure for some strange reason, because her voice was so calm and cool and I had my friends with me.

She said, "I think you're so beautiful and you would be such a great friend for my son Joey!"

Sylvia Robinson: The Mother of Hip-Hop

I responded, "Thank you so much," blushing at the same time, then I said, "I'm sure that's a compliment, but no thank you!" And started walking again but a lot faster!

She said in the same beautiful sultry voice, "Well, can you all just be friends? Maybe you can learn to like each other after you're friends for a while? He's right here, sitting in the back of the limousine!"

The other window in the back of the limousine opened completely and there he was, her handsome son, Joey. He was very shy but had a nice smile and said, "I would love to get to know you."

So that day Joey and I exchanged phone numbers. We talked on the phone every other day for a year. During that year, I only saw him maybe five times because he used to give these amazing parties up at his mansion in Englewood Cliffs, New Jersey. My brother was also a very good friend of his, and we became the best of friends, and ended up dating for five years! I dated him until I went off to college.

His family was my family and vice versa. Ms. Rob became my second mom, and she was so proud that she had literally found me for her son. We saw each other often, after school and on weekends.

But my fondest memory would be in the music studio, sitting side-by-side with her working all day and night with Joey and all her talents.

While Sylvia Robinson was recording in the studio at Sugar Hill Records in Englewood, New Jersey, she was also teaching us how to record music, and she would give a great deal of advice about producing and writing music. I spent countless hours – years – in that recording studio and learned a lot about how music is made.

I was literally in the studio when "Rappers Delight" was recorded in 1979 by the Sugarhill Gang, also later with Melle Mel, Grandmaster Flash & the Furious Five, Busta Rhymes, Angie Stone, and the list goes on and on.

Sylvia Robinson was determined to make Hip-Hop music legendary. She was a self-made singer and songwriter by her own right, but she saw talent in the Hip-Hop music world, because it was untapped, and she wanted the world to know how fascinating Hip-Hop music was, no matter what your age or race. It was also important for her initially to write and produce clean rap music lyrics to cater to a crossover type of audience.

At the time, everyone in the industry told her that Hip-Hop would never make it in America and they told her that it was only going to be trendy for a short time, but it still lives to this day!

Sylvia Robinson is the "Woman Behind the Mic," that started Hip-Hop and has had many famous Hip-Hop artists that are still recording today. She was one of the hardest working women in music that I have ever known personally. She was such an inspiration in my life and was part of my personal village of knowledge and taught me the art of music and creativity. She also taught me how to mix music notes with lyrics, how patience is a virtue in life, and to never give up on your dreams.

She is and will always be a pioneer in the music industry and the world needs to understand how important her role played in the music business and especially as a Black woman. She started the Hip-Hop culture and made it a universal language, and I'm so proud to have known her in my lifetime.

Hail to the Mother of Hip-Hop...Ms. Sylvia Robinson! She is missed and surely never forgotten. RIP, Sylvia Robinson.

Terri Ellis Ewing has a BA in Broadcast Journalism from Rutgers University. She started her career in sales and marketing at the IBM Corporation, and later worked in pharmacology at Sanofi Winthrop Pharmaceuticals, and later became an Oncology Specialist at Schering-Plough Pharmaceuticals. In her spare time, Terri has also pursued her dream as an actor, voice over artist, and now an author. Her upcoming book will be released sometime in 2024. Terri is married with two adult children and lives in Atlanta where she and her husband own and operate an automotive dealership.

Sylvia Robinson: The Mother of Hip-Hop

Terri and Joey

Mic Check 2

"I'm A Female Hip-Hop Pioneer"
~by~
Sweet Tee

It was a Tuesday night in the Spring of 1986, and I had just quit the group I had been in for a short time, the Glamour Girls. Feeling down but relieved, I needed something to lift my spirits, so I decided to head to the Latin Quarter, mid-town in New York City.

During the 1980s, the Latin Quarter on West 48th Street became a hub for emerging Hip-Hop artists and was known as the Club of Clubs. It was the place to be seen and played a significant role in the Golden Era of Hip-Hop in the mid-to-late '80s. The club was situated in midtown Manhattan and was known for hosting performances by many Hip-Hop artists who came from far and wide to showcase their talent on its stage. This iconic venue played a crucial role in shaping the Hip-Hop scene during the 1980s and left a lasting impact on the industry.

The Latin Quarter holds a special place in my heart. Once inside its walls, it was as if all the worries and problems of the outside world simply vanished. The Latin Quarter always had a way of making me feel better. As I walked in, the beats of Hip-Hop music immediately washed away my troubles. I grabbed a drink and navigated through the lively crowd, searching for a spot to unwind and enjoy the night.

As I settled in, a gentleman approached me and introduced himself as Hurby Azor, also known as Hurby Luv Bug. He told me that he recognized me, had seen me perform before, and expressed his desire to work with me. Little did he know that I had just left the Glamour Girls earlier that night, and I was eager to embark on a solo career. It was as if fate had brought us together at the perfect moment.

As the night wore on, the vibrant atmosphere and the company of my newfound collaborator filled me with excitement. When it was time to leave, Hurby kindly offered to drop me off at home. The events of the evening felt surreal, and I could hardly believe my luck. Sleep eluded me as I lay in bed, my mind racing with creative energy. As a writer, I needed a melody to compose a song, so I conjured up a bass line in my head and began to write. Once I had something I was happy with, I called Hurby's phone and left the song idea and the rhymes on his answering machine before finally drifting off to sleep.

The very next day, Hurby called me and we went to his house, where he had a small studio set up. We worked together on the music, and by the end of the session, we had a draft of what would become my first solo single, "It's My Beat." It was the beginning of a new chapter in my life, and I couldn't have been more thrilled.

I had now become a proud member of the esteemed Idol Makers Camp, which, at the time, boasted an impressive roster of talent, including Salt-N-Pepa, Kid 'n Play, Dana Dane, and now Sweet Tee. The camp continued to expand, incorporating other notable artists such as Kwamé, Antoinette, and others. It wasn't long before Hurby secured a record deal for me with the prestigious Profile Records.

I found myself in the company of legendary acts like Run-DMC, Dana Dane, Special Ed, King Sun & D Moet, and the rest of the esteemed Profile Records family. This new chapter in my career was an exhilarating experience, as I was surrounded by some of the most influential and talented individuals in the Hip-Hop industry.

In 1986, my first release from Profile Records, "It's My Beat," was just starting to gain traction. Hurby called me one day and told me I had a show booked at the Latin Quarter. It felt like everything had come full circle. I called Jazzy Joyce, my DJ at the time, and told her about the upcoming performance. I was ecstatic at the prospect of gracing the stage where everything had begun.

To make the night extra special, Hurby arranged for us to be chauffeured to Manhattan in a limousine. As we pulled up in front of the Latin Quarter, I noticed the marquee was dark, even though my name, Sweet Tee, and Jazzy Joyce's were displayed on it. There was a long line of people waiting to get in, stretching around the block. Hurby got out of the limo and banged on the club's front door. After what felt like an eternity, someone let him in. Jazzy Joyce and I sat in the limo and my heart was pounding with anticipation.

Hurby emerged from the club a few minutes later and explained that the lights were off because the venue was packed to capacity. They were waiting for us to arrive and could not let in any more people. It was an unbelievable feeling.

We said a quick prayer and entered the club. As we made our way to the stage and looked out at the sea of faces, I knew this was it. This was the moment I had been waiting for. That night, I left my heart on the stage, giving a performance I will never forget. It wasn't until I read Queen Latifah's book "Ladies First" that I discovered she had been in the audience that unforgettable night, just a young girl watching me perform.

That evening at the Latin Quarter marked the start of my solo career, a journey filled with passion, creativity, and a love for Hip-Hop. It was a night that would forever be etched in my memory, a testament to the power of music and the connections it can create. We had to return to perform in the Latin Quarter the next week because we could not forget those who didn't get into the club that night. This is just one story out of so many stories I hold dear from my Hip-Hop journey.

As a Hip-Hop pioneer, the 50th year of Hip-Hop holds a profound significance for me, as it represents the culmination of decades of passion, dedication, and hard work. The 50th year of Hip-Hop is an incredible milestone to celebrate and reflect upon the immense impact this genre has had on music, culture, and society. This art form has given a voice to countless individuals, including myself, empowering us to express our thoughts, feelings, and experiences in a way that resonates with people worldwide.

As we celebrate the 50th year of Hip-Hop, being a female pioneer in this genre holds a unique and empowering significance. Over the years, women in Hip-Hop have faced numerous challenges and barriers in a male-dominated industry. Still, our resilience, talent, and creativity have allowed us to break through and carve out a space for ourselves. This milestone is not only a testament to the strength and determination of female pioneers but also a celebration of the diversity and inclusivity that Hip-Hop has come to represent.

Looking back on the journey, it is humbling and inspiring to have been a part of the movement that paved the way for countless female artists who have followed in our footsteps. As a female pioneer, the 50th year of Hip-Hop serves as a reminder of the importance of our contributions and the responsibility we must continue in championing the voices of women in the genre. It is an opportunity to celebrate our progress while also acknowledging the work that still needs to be done to ensure equal representation and opportunities for all within the Hip-Hop community.

As we mark this significant milestone, we can take pride in female pioneers' impact on shaping the genre and inspiring future generations of artists. The 50th year of Hip-Hop is not only a celebration of the art form itself, but also a tribute to the trailblazing women who have defied expectations pushed boundaries, and helped redefine what it means to be a part of the Hip-Hop community.

As a pioneer, I take immense pride knowing that my contributions have helped define the genre and inspired countless individuals to find their voice through Hip-Hop. The 50th year of Hip-Hop is an opportunity to reflect on the past, appreciate the present, and envision the future of this ever-evolving genre. It is a chance to honor the legacy we have created and to continue fostering a culture of innovation, unity, and self-expression that will propel Hip-Hop to even greater heights in the years to come. The 50th anniversary serves as a poignant reminder of the impact we, as pioneers, have had in shaping the cultural landscape and paving the way for future generations of artists.

I'm A Female Hip-Hop Pioneer

Mic Check 3

"It's Not What You Know But Who You Represent"

~by~

Denise J. Brown

I owe my career in the entertainment industry to the Hip-Hop community!

Early in my career as an entertainment attorney, I invested in the Hip-Hop community, and the Hip-Hop community invested in me. Talent including Sean "Puffy" Combs, Salaam Remi, Busta Rhymes, Pharrell Williams, Sista Souljah, Foxy Brown, Notorious B.I.G., Pete Rock & C.L Smooth, Eddie F, Howie Tee, Little Shawn, Lost Boyz, and others understood their value and position. They understood mine. They were bold enough to say, "If you want me, you have to talk to Denise." My clients' talent and loyalty, along with my hard work ,paid off. When they blew up, so did my practice!

Notwithstanding my success, I was experiencing serious imposter syndrome. My biggest fear was that I was not experienced enough to manage a practice that was on fire. I had an epiphany during a meeting with Bert Padell, then the business manager to the stars. I will never forget what he told me: "Denise! It's not what you know but who you represent!" His philosophy was true in a sense. However, it was also true that I was who I represented.

As a young Black woman building a practice in a competitive field, I felt like I had a target on my back. If I had a client who was doing bad business, I would be accused of giving them bad advice. My clients' actions and missteps were a direct reflection on me. Accordingly, I was very careful about who I took on as a client, and I made sure that I operated with excellence.

A couple of anecdotes come to mind that describe my growth in the entertainment business. A record label president told my client who was on the verge of signing a record deal with his label, "Don't use Denise; she's not high-powered enough for this deal." One year later, that same record label president told another one of my clients that he was about to sign, "Don't use Denise; she's too high-powered for this deal"! I also remember a record label executive telling one of my clients that I was a "barracuda." Instead of that disparaging comment dissuading my client from using me, my client was proud and excited that I was viewed in that light by the head of his label!

Internationally renowned entertainment attorney Kendall Minter was my trainer and mentor. He took the time despite his very busy, very successful practice to make sure that I knew what I was doing. He made sure that I knew my way around entertainment industry agreements and that I was proficient in drafting and negotiating contracts. Powerhouse entertainment attorney Louise West was my North Star. When I came into the business, she was the only Black woman I knew who was practicing entertainment law on a high level. She was gracious and generous with her time, knowledge, and experience.

Sylvia Rhone, one of the most influential executives in the music industry, was my sponsor. She opened the door for me to become a partner at Mayer, Katz, Leibowitz & Roberts, then one of the top entertainment firms in New York. Her influence also led to my position as head of the Black Music Division at Warner Bros. Records. Howard Comart, another well-known entertainment business manager, was my cheerleader. He saw qualities in me that I did not see in myself. In the early years of my practice, he would tell me, "You're going to be big!" He also told me, "If you get in a room with a potential client, you are coming out of the room with that client.". Those words resonated with me then and throughout my career.

The pillars of my practice not only included doing excellent work and being careful about who I represented, they also included the adages: "No deal is better than a bad deal" and "The best client is an informed client." It was very important to me that my clients understood the deals that they were making, and I always made sure we talked through the terms before they signed on the dotted line. The entertainment business was exactly that: a business and a way to earn a good living to take care of themselves and their families.

I also never represented a client that I did not believe in creatively. Being a musician myself, I was able to use my "ear" as well as my intelligence to discern whether a client had potential to succeed in the business. I was also fearful that I would not represent a client properly if that client and I were not aligned creatively. Lastly, a sense of fairness was integral in every negotiation I handled. More often than not, the deal being negotiated involved the start of a relationship, and it was important that each party entered the relationship feeling like they each got what they bargained for. It would be a disaster for either party to enter the relationship feeling resentful of the other because of what occurred during the negotiation.

Like my clients, I was blessed to earn a living doing what I loved. My dream as a young woman was to be a classical concert pianist like Andre Watts. In addition to playing the piano, one of my favorite pastimes was listening to music and reading the album credits to learn who wrote the song and who produced, mixed, and mastered the record. Rather than following through with my original plan of attending a conservatory to study piano performance, I attended New York University and majored in the music business. This course of study allowed me to take music courses, business courses, and courses specifically geared toward the music business.

During my junior year, my college advisor, Richard Broderick, who was also chair of NYU's music business program, encouraged me to go to law school. He advised me that I would have more credibility and stability in the industry with a law degree. It was no coincidence that most of the presidents of the major record labels at that time were lawyers! When I told my parents that I was going to apply to law school, their response was, "Where is our daughter and what have you done with her?"

After earning a Bachelor of Science degree in the music business, I attended Brooklyn Law School. During my undergraduate and law school years, I interned in various departments at CBS Records (now Sony Music Entertainment). While there, several executives, including LeBaron Taylor, Mike Bernardo, Scott Folks, Steve Backer, Barry Levine, Walter Dean, Rand Hoffman, Gene Tarant, and LaVerne Perry were influential in my career. It was during these internships that I met Kendall Minter, for whom I went on to work, and producer Van Gibbs who became a client, along with his son, producer Salaam Remi. My time at CBS Records yielded long-lasting, impactful relationships.

Upon graduation from law school, I was given the opportunity of a lifetime to work for Reginald F. Lewis. At the time, he was not only the senior partner of a small corporate firm, Lewis & Clarkson, he was also the principal of TLC Group, a leveraged buy-out company. While I was there, he completed the acquisition of Beatrice International Foods, the largest leveraged buy-out acquisition in history at that point. As the only woman attorney at the firm and the company, I sharpened my negotiation skills. I also learned the mix between law and business. These skills proved invaluable in my entertainment practice.

I am proud of the practice that I was able to build across many music genres, representing a diverse range of talent, including the late Prince; Jon Hendricks (of Lambert, Hendricks and Ross); Ornette Coleman, a MacArthur Prize recipient and world-renowned jazz artist; gospel's John P. Kee; producer Rodney Jerkins; and R&B artist KEM. I am also grateful to have held my dream job: Running a record division. There is nothing like helping break a new artist, hearing your artists' records on the radio, or seeing them perform on stage before an adoring audience. Although my first love is music, my practice expanded into other areas of entertainment, including film, television, literary, and licensing.

In 2008, I decided to return to school. As a woman of faith, it became important to me that I increase my biblical knowledge and nurture a more intimate relationship with God. I enrolled in seminary. As I result, I have earned three more degrees, including a Doctorate in Biblical Studies. I am licensed and ordained as a minister.

I have always enjoyed mentoring young people who expressed a desire to work in the entertainment industry either on the creative or the business side. I now have an active role in doing so as an adjunct professor at my alma mater, NYU, and at Marymount Manhattan College. In 2018, I was inducted into the Black Entertainment and Sports Lawyers Association's Hall of Fame, and the following year I was honored to be awarded the Mike Bernardo Award by the Living Legends Foundation.

My advice to women who want to have a career in the entertainment business is to find someone who is doing exactly what you want to do and reach out to them! Study what they did to be successful and follow the trail they blazed. If you do not know exactly what you want to do in the industry, seek out informational interviews with people in the business to discover what area matches your skills and your interests. Internships are a must! As an intern, you can observe and learn different areas of the business, and, most importantly, you are able to develop relationships that will aid you throughout your career.

I am grateful to my clients for the privilege of representing them. I am also grateful to the many people in the entertainment industry who have had an impact on my career – too many to mention but they know who they are!

Denise J. Brown lives in the New York City area and is the mother of two children, Rahsaan and Tylese. She is also "Noni" to her 3-year-old granddaughter, Waverly. As an Adjunct Professor at NYUs Clive Davis Institute of Recorded Music and Marymount Manhattan College, Denise is living her best life as she is involved in the entertainment business, and ministry.

Mic Check 4

"Rap-It-Up"
~by~
Vikki Johnson

When I was growing up in South Florida, the Friday night weekly dance party called the "Jam Factory" could not come quick enough. Some Saturday nights I would go to the YMCA near my grandmother's house for the occasional dance party with my friends Karen, Mel and Natalie. We all loved to dance.

"David Deal Play Day" during the summer was another pivotal experience for me as a teenager. This particular summer, I was probably 13 years old and remember seeing The S.O.S. Band perform live at Sunland Park. I was enamored by their show. It was mesmerizing. It was super special because one of the lead singers, Fredi, was from my hometown AND we attended the same church. In that moment I knew I would somehow be in the music or entertainment industry.

A few years later, I officially started my career in the promotions department for WRBD (1490 AM) Gainesville, Florida. I was 15 years old working the concession stand at the neighborhood recreation center for the teen dance parties. I had a bird's eye view of everything and everybody. I would also listen daily to my cousin, Julian "Dr. J" Wright, who was an on-air personality for this same station.

Fast forward to my college days at Howard University (The Mecca) in Washington, D.C. (aka The Chocolate City). I was in the "School of C," as the Communications building was affectionately called. Part of

Photo Credit: Jackie Hicks for Fond Memories Photography

my graduation requirement was to complete an internship. I completed two. My first one was at RCA Records when Evelyn "Champagne" King was hot. My second internship was at Black Entertainment Television (BET) when Jamie Foster Brown (founder and editor of *Sister 2 Sister* Magazine) was the music director and Donnie Simpson along with Sherry Carter were hosting the show "Video Soul."

After graduating from HU in 1987, I went to work for Michael Jordan's sports agent, David Falk, for seven years. Shortly after leaving that job, I was in the mall and literally bumped into my BET internship supervisor, Sharon Strange Lewis. That was a God moment! She had left BET years earlier to work for other media companies but had just returned to launch the BET On Jazz channel and needed an assistant. I faxed her my résumé the next day. She hired me that week. That was the beginning of my 18-year career at the network.

I started with the jazz channel, then moved to BET Action PPV, then I serendipitously began working in affiliate marketing & sales. Eventually I worked in BET's marketing & promotions department, which was a lot of fun. I really enjoyed my job.

One day everything changed. God was definitely setting me up in ways I could not fathom or imagine. In this moment. however, it did not feel anything like a blessing. It felt like a war zone and very unsettling.

It was a perfectly normal BET day. You had to have worked there to understand. No two days were ever alike. After a couple hours, we all realized that our colleagues were being unexpectedly laid off. It was an emotionally difficult experience. I think many of us are still traumatized by that day, more than over two decades later. IT WAS HORRIBLE. None of us knew who was next. It appeared as if they were randomly coming to get people.

By the end of the day, layoffs appeared to stop. Those of us who remained were gathered into a space and told there was a major downsizing. A new organizational chart was distributed. There it was. I spotted my name above "RIU/CIC."

I asked, "What is that?"

Rap-It-Up

The response: "That's our new HIV/AIDS initiative and you are going to run it."

"WHAT?!!! Are you kidding me?" I knew nothing about that disease except that all the people I knew or had heard about who were diagnosed with it died quickly. I was terrified. HIV/AIDS was ravaging the Black community. One in every 50 people was contracting HIV, which was quickly progressing to full-blown AIDS. It was an epidemic. As I sit here reflecting, it actually felt much like a pandemic and the Black community needed an urgent response.

I came to work for a couple of weeks and just stared at my computer. The only other thing I did was flip through the gigantic, three-ring binder that was handed to me as "BET's new pro social campaign."

LOL! I guess God was like "let me help her because she is pitiful." The message at church the Sunday before this particular Monday shifted something in me. I received an infusion of courage and passion. I was ready to show up and use entertainment to educate.

The next day (Monday), I got a call from LaJoyce Brookshire inviting me to attend, on behalf of BET Networks, a Black Clergy & Media Roundtable to discuss our response to HIV/AIDS. I left that week-long meeting with new relationships, new partnerships, new friends, and a renewed sense or urgency to do something.

BET's campaign "Rap-It-Up (RIU)" became the blueprint for other networks/media to address this issue. Eventually, Sonya Lockett and Nneka Norville joined me as we became a team of three. For 13 years our efforts reached millions of people via our school curriculum, teen forums at middle/high schools around the country, public service announcements, a screenwriting competition, HIV testing initiatives, concerts, movies, sponsorships and partnerships with AIDS services organizations (ASOs), as well as local health departments. The campaign earned BET and the production team an Emmy and an NAACP Image Award.

A few notable HIV/AIDS warriors who added tremendous value to our work: Denise Stokes, Maria Davis, Hydeia Broadbent, Marvelyn Brown, Rae Lewis Thornton, Debra Fraser-Howze, Dr. Jeri Dyson, Dr. Rachel Ross, Dr. Scyatta Wallace, Dr. Theresa "Dr. T" McGill, and the unforgettable Sandra "Mama Mac" McDonald. There were SO many others.

Celebrity support was amazing, too. Talent like Sammie, Tank, Lamman Rucker, Mary J. Blige, comedian Joe Clair, Justine Love, Avant, Jade Novah, Soulja Boy, Monica, Jessica Reedy, Y'Anna Crawley, Skye Townsend, Sheryl Lee Ralph, celebrity makeup artist Kym Lee, and many, many more contributed to the campaign.

I am grateful to be part of history. We had a huge impact on Black culture. Our goal was to remove or, at a minimum, decrease the stigma associated with HIV/AIDS. We did that! The goal was to get people to "wrap it up" and we did just that. The message still resonates today: "Be safe. Be smart. Rap-It-Up." It's a wrap!

Dr. Vikki Johnson is a transformational speaker, chaplain, spiritual mentor to many, best-selling author and Founder of Soul Wealth LLC. Her daily podcast "The Soul Wealth Radio Show" is available on all podcast platforms and can also be heard live each day at 10AM EST on DCRadio.gov. With almost 40 years in the entertainment industry, she is an Emmy Award and NAACP Image Award winning media professional who worked at BET Networks for over 18 years. She currently serves in the Mayor's Office of Cable Television, Film, Music & Entertainment (OCTFME) for the District of Columbia on the film team and other special projects.

Vikki with Mary J. Blige

(L to R) Denise Stokes, AIDS Activist, Dr. Rachael Ross, MD, PhD, Board Certified Physician & Sexologist, Vikki Johnson, RIU Senior Manager, Sammie, R & B artist, Alesha Renee, BET On-Air Personality

Mic Check 5

"The Wealth of Hip-Hop Revealed"
~by~
Audra Washington-Madison

My impact on Hip-Hop spans from 1992 to 2005. As a music publisher, I held the responsibility and privilege of educating songwriters, artists, and producers about the significance of performance right royalties, music publishing, and the intricacies of deals. Music publishing is the lifeblood of the music industry, particularly for Black artists who often didn't reap the financial rewards of their creations due to stolen or involuntarily relinquished publishing rights. At the beginning of my career, I underestimated the importance of my role, but as I gained more knowledge about being a publisher, my commitment to serving Black music, especially in Hip-Hop, became crystal clear.

My mission has been to educate, inform, inspire, elevate, and be an unwavering supporter of Black culture, songwriters, producers, and Hip-Hop. I've worked tirelessly to clarify the entitlements related to songs, ownership, sharing of profits, impactful lyrics, production collaborations, and the care of legendary artists and their legacies. This commitment remains steadfast to ensure that these creatives receive not just influence and public admiration, but also the lasting financial security they deserve.

The process of translating studio discussions and artist interactions into proper title registrations and splits demands careful attention and mathematical precision. My contribution to Hip-Hop has always been centered on revealing the financial pathways, demonstrating the correct methods of monetization, and guiding artists toward earning their rightful dues.

My love affair with Hip-Hop began in 1984 when I heard Roxanne Shanté's "Roxanne's Revenge." As a young Black girl attending an all-girl Catholic high school in New York City, the song's empowering response to male disrespect resonated deeply. It was a defining moment that shifted my perspective, instilling in me the confidence to stand up against any form of mistreatment. Roxanne Shanté was the first to become my role model, inspiring me to embrace my strength and identity. It was like an "aha moment" that I did not have to, as a girl, take any sh** from anybody. Roxanne Shanté changed the trajectory of my posture. I was a petite 5-foot-1 girl raised by the streets of New York, and "Roxanne's Revenge" gave me grit and gumption to STAND 10 toes down without fear and with style.

Roxanne was my first fan girl experience: That edgy look, the bamboo earrings, the asymmetrical haircut, and her take-on-any-male-rapper-and-destroy-them ATTITUDE was when I first fell in love with Hip-Hop. Not only a lyrical savage, Roxanne also validated, at least to me, that it was okay to be a savage with the mouth to defend one's honor. My entire crew and all girls in New York City wanted to be Roxanne Shanté when the "Roxanne's Revenge" record was released. We simply could not get enough of her. Every time the song was played on WBLS it was electrifying to hear a female response like hers on the radio. No one had ever heard this type of response. "Roxanne's Revenge" was our mantra and we had Roxanne Shanté defending not only her crown but all US Black girls everywhere.

My journey in the Hip-Hop industry commenced in 1992 and extended to 1997 at the American Society of Composers, Authors, and Publishers (ASCAP)/ As the Director of Writer Relations for East Coast Urban Music, I created songwriting workshops and talent showcases around New York City and produced the highly anticipated annual ASCAP Rhythm & Blues Awards first conceived by my mentor, Ms. Vivian Scott-Chew, who was the first Black executive at ASCAP. I continued this path from 1997 to 2000 as the Creative Director for

EMI-Jobete Music Publishing. At EMI, I focused on the Motown (Jobete) Music catalog, seeking innovative ways to amplify its value and generate revenue, starting with the global recognition and production of the NFL's Half-Time Show celebration the 40th Anniversary of Berry Gordy and Motown Records.

My entry into the world of Hip-Hop was serendipitous. I started as an administrative assistant at ASCAP's New York office after graduating from historically Black Bennett College in Greensboro, North Carolina. My initial exposure allowed me to connect with industry professionals and build a network. Recognizing my passion and potential, Lisa Schmidt, the Executive Director of the New York office, promoted me to seek out emerging urban songwriters, artists, and producers, ensuring that their royalties were protected.

I traveled up and down the Eastern seaboard to sign not only the up-and-coming songwriters and artists like Mary J. Blige, Sean "Puffy" Combs, The Notorious B.I.G, 112, TOTAL, TLC, OutKast, Organized Noize, Missy Elliott, Timbaland, and others too many to name. I was also responsible for taking care of all the title registrations when they came in for filing from Uptown Records, DJ Eddie F's Untouchable Entertainment, Bad Boy Entertainment, Jermaine Dupri's So-So Def Records, Dallas Austin's Rowdy Records, Rough Riders Entertainment, Queen Latifah and Flavor Unit, Inc., MC Lyte, EPMD, Heavy D, Salt-N-Pepa, LL Cool J, and so many others. I was also the point of contact for legacy icons like Ashford &Simpson, Gwen Guthrie, the Marvin Gaye estate, Leon Ware (artists and co-writer with Marvin Gaye), Kashif, and all the Black writers and publishers that were ASCAP members, known and unknown.

The work that I was able to do and contribute to Hip-Hop was to marry and bridge the business of Hip-Hop and R&B, a duty the late songwriter/producer James Mtume charged to me accept. He said, "Audra, it is your responsibility to bring together two different generations so that they can collectively continue to learn and benefit off of each other; remember that it's always about the song – it's 50/50." I took that charge and continue to honor that responsibility to Black music and the Culture.

Reflecting on Hip-Hop's 50th anniversary, I'm overwhelmed by the global celebration. Witnessing the transformation of Hip-Hop from its origins to its current influential and multifaceted state fills me with awe. Hip-Hop has influenced not only music, but it has also become a 7.7-billion-dollar industry across all business sectors and countries.

Knowing that I've played a significant role in educating Hip-Hop creators about royalties and shaping the industry into the most popular genre of music in the United States makes me proud, humble, and immensely grateful.

Audra Washington-Madison is a trailblazing marketing dynamo, making history as the first woman of color to lead at the Maryland Jockey Club in its illustrious 280-year history. As the Director of Marketing, she orchestrates the magic behind the world-renowned Preakness Stakes, home to the second jewel of the Triple Crown. With a stellar career spanning two decades, Audra's expertise traverses diverse realms, from music and financial services to the exhilarating world of horse racing. She's an active member of prestigious professional organizations, and her accolades have graced the pages of Essence Magazine, The Hollywood Reporter, Billboard Magazine, *and more. Audra is married and has an adult daughter.*

The Wealth of Hip-Hop Revealed

(L to R) James "Jimmy Jam" Harris, his wife Lisa, Devante, Audra

(L to R) Mary J. Blige, Audra, ASCAP's Bill Brown

Mic Check 6

"Chronicling The Business of Hip-Hop"
~by~
Janine Coveney

I was raised in the South Bronx, Hip-Hop's universally acknowledged Motherland. I knew from a young age that I was going to be a writer, and I always loved music. The soundtrack of my teen years was filled with funk, R&B, and disco, and I had a front-row seat to watching how the DJs and Jamaican toasters of the house parties, street jams, and club getdowns honed their rapping skills on the microphone. By the late '70s they had pushed their clever rhyme style forward until the words of the newly minted MCs became the very grooves we thirsted for. When I got to my second year at Simmons College in Boston, "Rapper's Delight" had taken over the national airwaves. There was no longer any question. Hip-Hop was an undeniable force.

After graduating, returning to New York City, and cycling through gigs at Scholastic, *Essence* Magazine, and an unfortunate stint at the New York City Housing Authority (NYCHA), I was thrilled when I was hired as a copy editor at music business weekly *Billboard* in the late 1980s. Within two years I was the Senior Copy Editor and a writing contributor, interviewing and writing about artists and business for various sections of the magazine.

In June 1989 I interviewed newly minted star LL Cool J on a school bus parked in front of the Def Jam offices in lower Manhattan. LL was about to go on a national tour and as I recall, traveling to each show in a school bus was part of the gimmick. In consulting my scribbled notes from our session – which I still have -- I called it a "sham, waste-of-time interview" and labeled him "boneheaded but undeniably talented." He was still very young at the time, not yet the mature media master he has since become; his responses then were weak and full of the expected street jargon that didn't add up to a full, quotable sentence. After insisting that I should come on tour with him, a sentiment about which he seemed entirely serious, I ended the interview and prepared to leave. But then he threatened not to let me off the bus! It took a few minutes for LL to stop blocking my path with a lascivious grin and let me pull open those folding metal doors to the street.

As soon as I got back to the *Billboard* offices off of Times Square, I was called into an interview with the magazine's publisher. Within days I was named Black Music Editor, succeeding Nelson George, who had helped develop my expertise in writing about the music. As a new editor at *Billboard*, I had landed neck deep into a music industry where the ascendance of Hip-Hop was already in progress at a head-spinning rate.

A plethora of independent record labels and new major label divisions had sprung up after it was clear that Hip-Hop and rap were the music of the moment, and a whole new world of artists skilled at spitting rhymes were being pitched for coverage. Hip-Hop was tipping the entire music industry on its ear, not only in terms of how the music sounded, but in terms of the social, political, cultural, and visual elements it injected into the conversation about entertainment. Working at *Billboard*, being a music trade magazine focusing on the business aspects of the industry, meant I had to report on new trends – both the successes and failures – in music production, promotional campaigns, video production, radio programming, touring, and branding. How were the labels winning? How were the artists connecting?

The transition to my new role was effective with the July 22nd issue. My feature story for the section is a piece I penned about Kool Moe Dee after interviewing him and several record executives, titled "Kool Moe Dee Raps Up Another Album/ *Social Consciousness Rules This 'King'*." Meanwhile, the Top Ten titles on the *Billboard* Top Black Albums chart for that week: LL Cool J's *Walking With A Panther* at No. 1; *The Adventures of Slick Rick* at Number 2; Kool Moe Dee's *Knowledge*

Is King at No. 4; MC Hammer's *Let's Get It Started* at No. 6 and De La Soul's *3 Feet High And Rising* at No. 8. In that same issue, Slick Rick had the inside cover gatefold ad from Def Jam/Columbia Records.

In August, my second month on the job, I teamed with a fellow writer to pen the front-page story "Rappers Gain More Staying Power," acknowledging the dominance of gold and platinum-certified artists like LL Cool J and Run DMC. They were no longer seen as novelties making one-off 12-inch singles, but as full-fledged creative artists into whom labels now sunk big artist-development dollars.

Hip-Hop IS Black Music, and that was my beat. I interviewed dozens of rappers about the music they made and what inspired them to make it. I also interviewed their managers, label executives, and radio programmers, sharing their views on how the music was part of the culture, how it should best be promoted, and how (and whether) it should be played on the radio. The issue of censorship and bleeping certain words for airplay was a major issue for radio programmers during those days, caught between playing what their audiences wanted to hear and the ire of conservative listeners and the legal reach of the FCC's broadcast rules.

As Public Enemy's Chuck D famously noted, Rap was Black America's CNN, and despite criticism about its content, it told the truth of the Black Experience for many. So when L.A. burned in the 1992 riots in reaction to the Rodney King verdict, my column was titled "We Told You So: Rap Acts Saw Writing On The Wall." When Ice-T ventured into rock and released the track "Cop Killer," I was part of the media covering the firestorm about violent lyrics, censorship, and free speech.

Interviewing artists was my favorite part of the gig, and with weekly deadlines, I alternated duties with contributing writers. Among those I sat with, a few Hip-Hop-related stories stick in my mind. While I had dozens of positive interactions with an array of popular Hip-Hop artists, those weren't necessarily the memorable ones! I think it wasn't just the fact that I was a woman, it was also my demeanor – maybe a bit too buttoned-up and librarian-ish – that spawned frequent teasing as well as flirting from male artists.

I remember doing an interview with rapper Big Daddy Kane at the NYC offices of Warner Bros. Records, which was distributing the Cold Chillin' label. Publicist Gene Shelton ordered us lunch and left us alone in a conference room. Kane was promoting his 1990 album *A Taste of Chocolate* at the time, and as I recall the fall weather was a bit nippy. I wore a coat, jacket, wrap blouse, skirt, tights, and boots. I was partial to wearing hats in those days, so I was also sporting a black velvet broad-brimmed porkpie style that I'd picked up at a Manhattan street vendor. With his deep brown skin, bedroom eyes, and mellifluous baritone, Kane emanated sex appeal and he knew it. As our chat got under way, he said playfully, "You have on too many clothes, girl. You need to take something off." Though I knew he was being facetious, I was taken aback. Within minutes of our sitting down, he had admired my hat, so in response I took that off and said that was all he was getting! He asked to try it on and I acceded. With my velvet hat on his head, Kane continued the rest of the interview. He looked damned good in that hat and I almost left the building without it.

In those days, female rap artists were far and few between, though the successes of Queen Latifah, MC Lyte, and Salt-N-Pepa (my favorite interviews) prompted labels to sign on a plethora of female talents who became one-hit wonders until the likes of Lil Kim, Foxy Brown, and Eve gained traction and notoriety years later. It was fascinating to interview so many women who were dedicated to Hip-Hop, because their demeanors, styles, and approaches were so different. I made it a point to collect and keep the press packages for every female rap artists I came across, a file I still possess: Bahamadia, Lady of Rage, Hoes With Attitude, Yo-Yo, Queen Pen, MC Trouble, Isis, Charli Baltimore, Da Brat, Missy Elliott and so many more. These women pushed hard in a male dominated landscape to get their turn at the mic.

During a trip to Miami for a music business conference, I was invited to an off-site party at a local South Beach mansion. I don't remember whose place it was, or why we were there. What I do remember is that there were more than a few rappers in attendance, including Tupac Shakur. The grounds of the mansion included a tennis court, and after wandering outside and chatting briefly, we briefly banged a few balls back and forth over the net under a bright sun. What I remember about Pac was his enormous charisma and intelligence. The side of him that he revealed to me was smooth sensitivity and crackling smarts. Later on I would describe him by saying "that boy can charm the birds out of the trees." It wasn't a formal interview, and I never did sit him down for a one-on-one on the record. His talent as a lyricist and rapper were undeniable, and that energy easily translated on the screen in his film roles. It was just strange to witness the full expression of his talents and emotions in real life – so brilliant, thoughtful, and warm, but also volatile, self-destructive, aggressive, and raw. I was devastated like the rest of the world when I learned that he was murdered in Las Vegas. He was singularly talented.

The rise of Hip-Hop was so profound and so ... BIG ... that *Billboard* hired writer and contributor Havelock Nelson as its first Rap Music Editor in 1991. Havelock ended up covering the lion's share of the news and artists happening in the Hip-Hop sphere, leaving me to the burgeoning neo-soul movement, the rise of reggaeton, the expanding smooth jazz market, and more.

I left *Billboard* in May of 1993 and joined Arista Records as a product manager. In my ten months there I worked with Arista's Hip-Hop-oriented distributed labels: Sean "Puff Daddy" Combs' Bad Boy and producer Dallas Austin's Rowdy Records. And years later, after moving to the West Coast, I covered Hip-Hop again for the trade magazines *Billboard R&B Airplay Monitor* and *The Gavin Report* – both publications that were later discontinued.

When Hip-Hop was birthed into the world, I was a witness, a bystander, an observer and ultimately a chronicler. If there is something, anything, that I am proud to have contributed to the culture, it is probably the coverage of Hip-Hop in several major music trade magazines. Talking to artists about why and how they make the music, and why Hip-Hop is so important, and actually noting how it changed the business of music was thrilling. To see Hip-Hop stand 50 years strong is a triumph for them and for African-descended people not only in America, where it was born, but across the globe.

Janine M. Coveney is a writer and editor with more than three decades of experience. Coveney's résumé includes serving as jazz and urban radio news manager for Launch/Yahoo!; founding managing editor of Billboard's R&B Airplay Monitor; *R&B Music Editor of* Billboard; *Careers Editor of* Essence; *publicity director for A&M Records' Perspective label; and product management & marketing associate for Arista Records, shepherding the careers of Whitney Houston, Toni Braxton, Usher, and others. From 2013 to 2016 she was the content & communications manager for the advocacy division of The Recording Academy (The GRAMMYs) in Washington, D.C. She also hosts the classic movie fan podcast The Words On Flicks Show. Most recently, she served as the Head Writer for the inaugural Jazz Music Awards, held October 2022 in Atlanta.*

Janine with LL Cool J in Orlando, 1998

Chronicling The Business of Hip-Hop

Janine with Kurupt of Tha Dogg Pound

Janine with MC Hammer

Mic Check 7

"Makeup Artistry: A Path to Privilege"
~by~
Eleanora Winslow

As the first African American makeup artist in the New York Union of Makeup Artists and Hairstylists, I was blessed and highly favored to be gifted with a craft that was critical and crucial to the esthetics of cinematography, especially during the time which more films were being produced and portrayed by individuals of melanated hues.

I was affectionately known as "Ms. Ellie" in the motion picture film industry. For more than 25 years, upon every script presented to me – which included artists of this genre – I learned up close and personal about the culture of Hip-Hop. I had the honor and privilege of working with Tupac, Queen Latifah, Ice-T, and Busta Rhymes, just to name a few.

I was privy to the language, the lifestyle, the message being conveyed. and the very heartbeat of a community of individuals who were brilliantly skilled with the capacity to artistically express themselves in a manner that could be so proficiently translated to film. Each experience was unique, and every performance allowed the artist to bring his or her individual creativity to a production designed to engage their diehard fans and win a new audience on a bigger-than-life screen with entertainment, excitement, mystery, and great storytelling.

The '90s was a decade of introduction to and exposure for Hip-Hop culture. The artform was a showcase for these artists' application of expression and implementation of talent, demonstrating their ability to appeal to an entire generation. These Hip-Hop stars already had an established and loyal audience that guaranteed filled seats in movie theaters all over the country.

Working with Ice-T on *New Jack City* (1991), Queen Latifah on *Jungle Fever* (1991), Busta Rhymes on *Who's The Man?* (1993), and Tupac on *Above The Rim* (1994) were the specific films that benefitted from the contributions made by the above-mentioned artists. These films are culture classics today and can, therefore, still be appreciated decades later by an audience of their generation. Many who frequently visited the movie theater have chosen to pursue various careers in this industry as a result of seeing someone who looks like them in front of the camera or working behind the scenes.

Some of the other Hip-Hop artists of whom I have had the pleasure of working with were Ginuwine on *Juwanna Man* (2002) , Treach on *First Time Felon* (1997) and Mos Def on *Bamboozled* (2000).

This was the process: When the film was in pre-production, I would be contacted by the production manager, who was given my name by recommendation from a producer, director, or actor. I would then be informed of the nature of the film, the location of the filming, the duration of the filming, and the position being offered to me, which was either "Makeup Department Head" or "Star Request." If I was interested, a script would be mailed to me to read. I would then respond and contract negotiations would begin. I realized very early on that this is an industry of privilege. I also knew the importance of maintaining a spirit of excellence and professionalism in my conduct as well as demonstrating my competence to execute the desired result expected by those who had employed me.

One of my most memorable work experiences was during the time I worked with Tupac on *Above The Rim*. He was very professional, courteous, kind, and compliant. The script required a long scar to be created on one side of his face as a part of the character he portrayed. A life face cast molded by plaster was made by another special effects makeup artist which resulted in producing a scar that would be contoured to Tupac's bone structure and jaw line. The scar was made of clear plastic strips which I had to secure on his face and then match it to his skin tone. The process of the application took about fifteen minutes. He was so proud of it that he would not permit me to remove it at the end of the day's filming. He insisted on wearing it over the weekend and I would just replace it with a fresh one when we resumed filming on Monday.

He approached me one day in the makeup trailer and said, "Ms. Ellie, I have only one song of mine that I would like for you to listen to." It was "Dear Mama." The song had not been released to the public at that time.

I was very touched by the level of respect and consideration he displayed towards me as a mother figure, which clearly indicated that his upbringing was deeply ingrained within his soul and spirit. I always sensed that he was destined for greatness and was socially and politically ahead of his time. He was indeed an old soul, wise beyond his years. I am grateful for having had the opportunity to spend quality time in his company. His contribution to the Hip-Hop community has left an indelible imprint upon the hearts of masses.

Before I was accepted into the Makeup Artist and Hairstylist Union, my area of expertise had been in the Beauty Industry, working with models for magazines, runway fashion shows, beauty pageants, television makeovers, editorials, grooming politicians for campaign commercials, etc. However, to become a member of the union, the practical exam required that one would be able to make bald caps, cuts, scars, bruises, burns, black eyes, bullet holes, stitches, and hand lay a beard and sideburns. I attended seminars and took courses with other award-winning makeup artists, sometimes, spending hours in a studio to hone my craft.

The film that my signature is attached to the most is that of the mime faces I designed for the movie *Dead Presidents* (1995) Brinks truck robbery scene. After that film, I was asked to duplicate that look for an episode of the series *New York Undercover*.

Having been retired from the industry for more than a decade. I returned to school, earned and received my Bachelors and Master's

Degree in Theological Studies as well as having been a recipient of an Honorary Doctorate of Divinity as a result of my participation in the implementation of seminars, crusades, workshops and church services conducted in Ghana, West Africa.

Interestingly enough, when I shared with some of my colleagues that I was in full time ministry, the response from them was, "Miss Ellie, you have always been a preacher!" More times than I can remember, I was asked to pray for someone in my makeup chair or on set before filming. Since having left the Film Industry, God has been using my voice to help transform mankind from the inside and for that I am deeply humbled and eternally grateful.

Apostle Eleanora Winslow has a Bachelor's and Master's Degree in Theological Studies and is currently Assistant Pastor at Living Word Christian International Assembly under the leadership of Rev. Dr. Michael Darko in The Bronx, New York. Known as an intense Prayer Warrior, Apostle Winslow intercedes for the lost, the back-slidden, the downtrodden, the wounded, the broken-hearted, the disenfranchised, and confused persons. Her two passions are that the lost will be saved, and for those who are saved to walk in the power, dominion, and authority they have been given through the death, burial, resurrection, and ascension of our Lord and Savior Jesus Christ. I am the published author of DEVOURED BY PASSION: Determined To DO My Destiny. *She enjoys spending time in Los Angeles with her actor son and daughter-in-love, a classical singer, and her two grandchildren.*

Makeup Artistry: A Path to Privilege

Tupac's scar in "Above The Rim" created by Eleanora Winslow

Mic Check 8

"U.N.I.T.Y.: My PR Journey with The Queen"
~by~
Gwendolyn Quinn

Throughout my career, I have been fortunate to work with artists in various genres of music including R&B, gospel, jazz, blues, opera and classical, and Hip-Hop. Queen Latifah and Diddy were two of the biggest Hip-Hop artists as well as two of the most commercially successful artists that I worked with during my career in the recording industry.

As we celebrate 50 years of Hip-Hop, it is important to note that Queen Latifah's 35-year career is historic and iconic. I knew from day one, when I heard her first album *All Hail The Queen* featuring her mega-hit "Ladies First," that Dana Elaine Owens was destined for superstardom. What I didn't know was that I would share and be a part of her pioneering success as a recording artist, actor, and business leader.

Queen Latifah was creating Black Girl Magic before it became popular. I was fortunate to work with her during some of the earliest milestones in her career, especially the year 1993, which was a significant year for her. It was thirty years ago when she released her groundbreaking album *Black Reign* featuring the female anthem, "U.N.I.T.Y., Who You Callin' A Bitch?," for which she won a Grammy Award. In 1993, she began co-starring in Fox's hit sitcom *Living Single*. From there, she has starred in a string of movies, hosted a television talk show, authored a book, secured brand and endorsement deals, founded

Photo Credit: Matthew Jordan Smith

and heads a film and television production company, released more albums, and has been the recipient of countless awards and honors.

My career in Hip-Hop started in 1990 as a publicity coordinator at Mercury Records, which was part of the music conglomerate PolyGram. The rap roster included Ed O.G. & Da Bulldogs and Black Sheep. The mainstream urban roster included Tony! Toni! Toné!, Oleta Adams, Brian McKnight, Jon Lucien, Angela Winbush, and Third World. After six months, I lost my first label job at Mercury, and for nearly three years, I worked as a legal secretary at Coudert Brothers LLP, an international law firm, through a temporary employment agency. After two years at the law firm, I became discouraged about returning to the recording industry.

One day, music executive Jackie Rhinehart, who had hired me for my first record label position, phoned and said she recommended me for a publicity position. She had been offered the same position by Shakim Compere, the CEO of Flavor Unit Entertainment, and had to decline the offer because she had just accepted a job with Hiriam Hicks' management company in Philadelphia. My initial response to her was, "I don't want to work with a roster of Hip-Hop artists." Jackie's response was, "Girl, you better go to that interview and get that job because no one has offered you anything in the past few years." Don't get me wrong, I love Hip-Hop, but I grew up on classic R&B and I wanted to work with a diverse range of artists, as I had at Mercury Records.

Her words reverberated in my psyche. Shortly thereafter, I met with Flavor Unit Entertainment's CEO Shakim and Charm Warren, who was hired as the president to run the newly formed label, Favor Unit Records. I accepted the position of the National Director of Publicity for Flavor Unit Entertainment, which included Flavor Unit Management, both founded by Queen Latifah and Shakim. I commuted daily from the Clinton Hill section of Brooklyn to Jersey City, New Jersey. The Flavor Unit offices were in a renovated firehouse, located at 155 Morgan Street.

The label's roster included Zhané, The Flavor Unit MCs, Bigga Sistas, and The Almighty RSO, founded by then-group leader Ray

Dog, publicly known as Ray Benzino. Our four-member team included Charm Warren, Kobie Brown, and the late Glenn "G-Man" Holt. Flavor Unit Records was distributed by Epic Records, and we worked closely with their executive team, which included the music industry legends Hank Caldwell, La'Verne Perry-Kennedy, and Diane Blankumsee.

On the management side, I reported to Shakim. The artists on the management roster included Queen Latifah, Naughty By Nature, D-Nice, Black Sheep, Fu-Schnickens, Freddie Foxx, Nikki D, LaShaun, DJ Mark, The 45 King; Latee, and the late Apache. The management team included Lynn Scott, Rebekah Foster, Shirley Bell, Kathryn Khan, Danielle Stennett-Neris, Billy Allrich, and Paul Compere.

Early in my tenure, I mainly worked with Latifah and Naughty By Nature, who had current projects released and were still signed to Tommy Boy Records. Latifah's recording career was well established through Tommy Boy under the leadership of Tom Silverman and Monica Lynch, and publicist Laura Hines.

In 1993, Flavor Unit Records released its debut album, *Roll Wit Tha Flavor*, and Latifah appeared on the first single of the same title, which also featured the Flavor Unit MCs, and included Naughty By Nature, Black Sheep, Fu-Schnickens, Freddie Foxx, D-Nice, with a special guest appearance by the late Heavy D. My first major press booking was securing the Flavor Unit MCs on *The Arsenio Hall Show*, which was during the time he had exited the late-night show. The compilation album featured 16 songs including the international anthem "Hey Mr. DJ," performed by the new R&B duo Zhané, produced by Kay Gee of Naughty By Nature. I also secured my second *Essence* magazine cover with the group's Renee and Jean; that issue was one of the magazine's biggest sellers to date.

Shortly thereafter, Latifah moved to Motown Records, which was under the leadership of the late Jheryl Busby with the label's senior executive team headed by Steve McKeever. The PR team that I coordinated with included Michael Mitchell, Gwendolyn Priestley, and Christopher Cathcart. In 1993, Latifah also co-starred in *Living*

Single for five seasons in the role of Khadijah James, alongside Kim Fields, Kim Coles, Erika Alexander, John Henton, T.C. Carson, and Mel Jackson; executive produced by Yvette Lee Bowser.

Before arriving at Flavor Unit, Latifah lost her older brother, Lancelot, Jr., who was killed in an accident involving a motorcycle in 1992. Though her star was rising in music, television, and film, she was mourning the death of her brother and having difficulty coping with her newfound success. Her mother, Rita Owens, was her rock, along with Shakim. Everyone who surrounded her did their best to help her process her grief and work through her pain.

One day, I broke protocol and had a talk with Rita, who was affectionately known as Ms. O., who had an office at Flavor Unit. Ms. O was a teacher and would come to the office regularly after school. I shared with her that Latifah was turning down major media opportunities and she said, "Gwen, if Dana turns down any important press interviews, I want you to let me know." And from that point on, I informed her when Latifah was not responding or cooperating. On numerous occasions, Ms. O talked with her daughter and as a result, many interviews and press days were saved because of her intervention. I knew Latifah was still grieving about Lance and was still having a difficult time processing her loss. I was caught between a rock and a hard place because during that phase of her career, it was important for her to secure some of those big media looks. I'm not sure if she knew that I talked to her mother, but I had to do something. Ms. O was a fixer. She was also the resident counselor, and I talked with her about non-related work issues. She was easy to talk with and I shared a lot with her. Many years later, in 2018, I was heartbroken when she passed. I could not imagine what Latifah was going through. She was so close to her mother.

In 1993, I became Latifah's exclusive publicist, coordinating all her publicity interviews and appearances with the Fox Network and the record label. I traveled back and forth to Los Angeles when she relocated there to tape *Living Single*. She released her Motown debut album *Black Reign*, which featured her female anthem "U.N.I.T.Y. -- Who You Callin' A Bitch?" On her CD packaging, I remember being credited as the "Cover Girl," because I had secured numerous magazine covers for her, including her first for *Essence* (and my first *Essence* cover as a publicist) during that momentous time of her career. Thinking back, I would not have been able to do it without Ms. O.

After more than four years at the company, I decided that it was time to move on so that I could learn more about the field of public relations. Shakim and Latifah were great bosses and they were good to me. Yet I wanted be a better publicist and I wanted to work in a larger publicity department with other publicists. I had already proven to myself that I could do the job.

After I left the company, every time we had an encounter, Latifah remembered and communicated with me as though it was yesterday, old times. She showed me so much love.

There are so many things that I love about Dana, as I often called her interchangeably with Latifah. Her confidence and self-love; her influence on young girls and women across the globe; her impact on music, arts, and culture; her loyalty to family, friends, and community. She is truly one of the best that the Hip-Hop community has produced and I am proud to have worked with her.

Celebrating more than 30 years as one of the independent public relations leaders, Gwendolyn Quinn established Gwendolyn Quinn Public Relations, a full-service publicity and marketing firm that specializes in developing media strategies, coordinating special events, and brand development for clients who span the worlds of entertainment, performing arts, corporate, not-for-profit, faith-based, and the visual/fine arts. She is a multiple award-winning communications strategist and consultant. Her career in public relations has paired her with some of the industry's brightest stars in music, including the late Aretha Franklin, Whitney Houston, and Prince, as well as Chaka Khan, Queen Latifah, Sean "Diddy" Combs, The Isley Brothers, Deborah Cox, Bishop T.D. Jakes, Kirk Franklin, Andraé Crouch,

Karen Clark Sheard, and countless others. Currently, Quinn handles public relations and communications for the Estate of Whitney E. Houston and other music and entertainment clients. She is the founder of Africa54, a lifestyle company. She is the co-executive of the Jazz Music Awards. Quinn is a board member of the Living Legends Foundation, a member of The Recording Academy, and a voting member of the Voice Arts Awards.

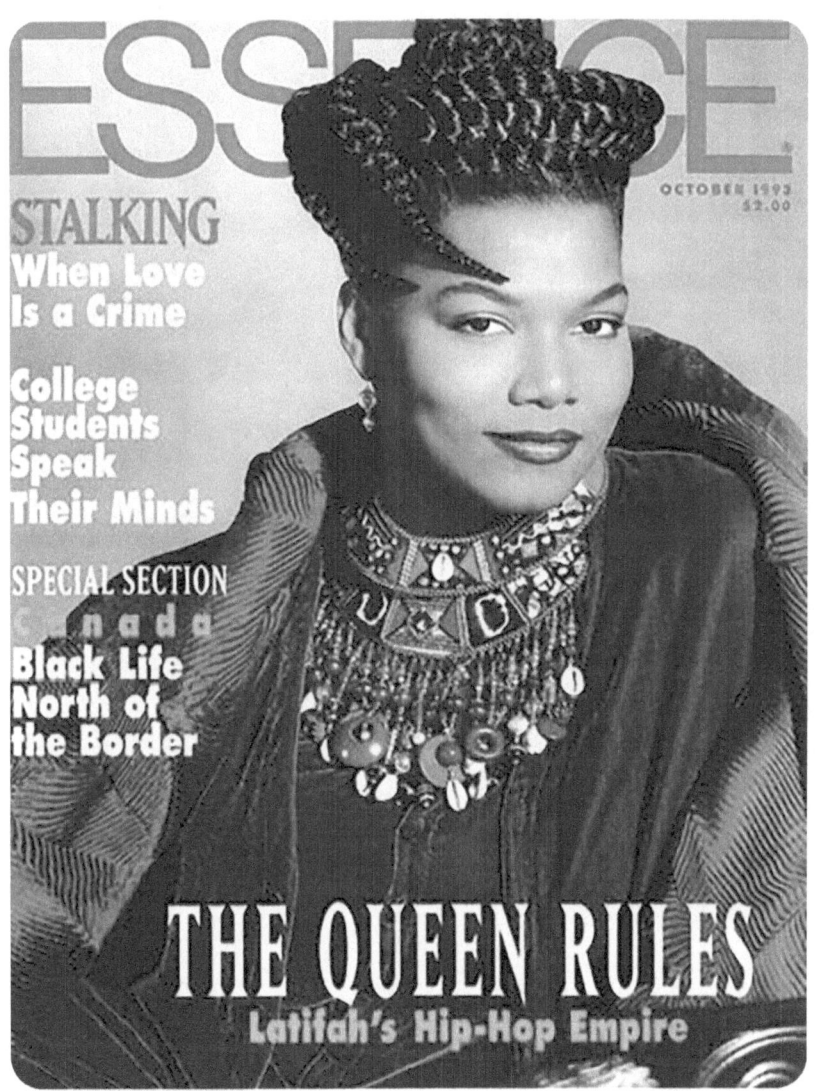

Gwendolyn's cover placement of Queen Latifah

Mic Check 9

"Taking Hip-Hop By Storm"
~by~
Pamela Crockett

The year was 1979 and it was on! Back when New York City's Tower Records – and, more relevant, Birdell Records – was a thing, my father came home with a fresh batch of albums. Unable to contain himself, he was fumbling with the bag and the turntable simultaneously, saying "You have to hear this one!" Beat started bumping and in comes "King Tim III" by the Fatback Band.

WHAT??????!!!!!!!! We went crazy. CRAZZZZZZZZZEEE!

And he wasn't done. He said, "Now check this out," and it was "Rapper's Delight." I thought I was the greatest dancer, or at least in the top two based on Sister Sledge. So, I'm doing the Spank and the Flintstone, going all in, listening to the mix of "Good Times" by Chic. They were slamming them beats like I was playing handball and that was before one word dropped. At that moment, I realized whatever I did in life, it would involve music and entertainment. To be a part of what came to be cemented as Hip-Hop was beyond a dream! And what a dream! Hip-Hop has allowed me to live.

I joined the Hip-Hop world officially as a professional almost three decades ago, dating back single-handedly to my "brother" Wayne Barrow. Wayne, along with Mark Pitts, made up By Storm Entertainment, the management team for the Notorious B.I.G; he ushered me into the Hip-Hop entertainment world in royal fashion. It is important for me to recognize him as I've always assumed he knew how much he means to me. I need him and anyone else to know he was the person who shaped my career and gave me the autonomy to live the life I desired to live and raise my children hands-on. So, cheers to Wayne Barrow as we approach a friendship that has lasted as long as Hip-Hop.

Denise Barrow –Wayne's real sister – is one of my best friends. When Wayne finished his valiant service to our country in the military and was ready to start his professional career, I had recently graduated from the University of Michigan Law School. Knowing my desire to be in sports and entertainment, Denise said, "You need to get with Wayne." I brushed him off for a long time as Denise was the proxy. But we were together one day and Wayne simply asked me if I wanted to "get in the game." I didn't think he was serious, but he was more than that. He had a vision on how he planned on taking the industry "by storm." We formed an informal partnership of sorts and Wayne promised to get me into the business in a meaningful way.

True to his word, I found myself in Virginia Beach, Virginia, and it changed my entire life. Virginia Beach, the Future scene, and producer Teddy Riley's world was unreal. As a young lady – attorney or otherwise – it was unbelievable being present when and where they were recording Michael Jackson's "Remember the Time," and "In the Closet," as well as Wreckx-N-Effect's "Rump Shaker" before they came to life.

How was this possible? Not thinking about advancing my career, I was still on my "greatest dancer" game and simply loving the scene. But Wayne kept saying, "I have so much more for you, Sis." Turns out he would become my all-access pass.

One day, Wayne asked me to meet him uptown. Dressed in my baddest lime-green, gold-button-down dress and carrying a top-notch briefcase, I hopped on the A train to 125th Street and walked a few short blocks to my destination. I was the first one there, so I took a seat on the bench waiting for my next introduction. And then it all crystalized. The smoothest voice on vinyl emerged in the courtyard as one-third of Wreckx-N-Effect. It felt like the largest speaker was blasting, "All I wanna do is zoom-a-zoom-zoom-zoom, Yeah . . ." It was Aqil "A-Plus" Davidson. But the music in my head was getting louder and all I could remember him saying was, "You're the only lawyer that ever came uptown to meet me. I gotta make you a part of the team." So, there I was with a potential major client – along with Wayne Barrow, my music mogul in the making – in whatever capacity they would have me. It opened a magical door as I was now related to two powerbrokers. Eclipsing the likelihood of pure chance or coincidence, I was now in the game.

Riding back downtown on the A train was a blur as I now had a platinum rapper and a manager representing who we knew would become the greatest solo rapper of all time. And I will forever be indebted, as not many people in that tax bracket were willing to take a chance on a young sister from Brooklyn.

In the time immediately following that, I felt like Hip-Hop was an urban IPO. Every place I went, we had permeated all facets of life from music to television and film to literary publishing to sports to fashion to cosmetology. If it involved Hip-Hop artists, they brought us along en masse. I recall one deal with an artist and another lawyer, even younger than myself, on our side. When the other parties showed up, they had a look of bewilderment on their faces. I answered for them: "You're wondering where are the adults?" I raised my hand and replied, "I'm it!" He apologized and I assured him no offense taken. He then revealed in his entire life he had never seen a major transaction for that amount of money where all the people in charge were young African-American women. It had become so common for me, I didn't think much about it.

Hip-Hop was us! And I was a part of major deals: ten million dollars here; boarding private jets; traveling first-class; yacht parties; *Ebony* Magazine "Super Singles Accomplished and Available" (July 1997 issue); greenlighting and redlighting, almost like the game I played as a child. When I went to concerts, I walked backstage with authority. When I needed tickets, I could expect to sit a row ahead of the Vice President and the Secret Service (true story). For all of us engaged in that era, it was truly all about US: Our music, our people, our culture, and our movement. It's hard today to wrap my head around the fact that, as all of this was unfolding, I was usually the oldest person in the room and I was barely 30.

Happy 50th Birthday, Hip-Hop! Like the young, bold African-American artists who launched and carried you, you were not supposed to make it! But you did, in magical fashion!

Pamela Crockettt, an Entertainment & Sports Consultant based in the DMV area, extends her service nationally. As the CEO of The Brand Collective Group, she specializes in curating Name Image and Likeness (NIL) opportunities for student athletes, emphasizing Diversity, Equity and Inclusion (DEI) and Title IX considerations. In addition to her consultancy work, Pamela is a credited movie producer, boasting two successful credits in 2023. Beyond her professional accomplishments, she takes pride in being the dedicated mother of Jeryne (an attorney); Jahre (currently pursuing a Master's Degree in Social Work); and Jerlan (working towards a Bachelor's Degree in History). Notably each of them demonstrated exceptional commitment as student athletes while pursuing their respective degrees.

(L to R) Pamela with Wayne and Denise Barrow

Mic Check 10

"Launching The Notorious V.I.P."
~by~
LaJoyce Brookshire

It was an extremely busy afternoon. As the Director of Publicity at Arista Records, as usual I was wrangling the 250 calls I received daily, screened by my assistant Peri. In that seat I handled "The Queen of Soul" Miss Aretha Franklin, Whitney Houston, Toni Braxton, Deborah Cox, Usher, 112, Faith Evans, Monica, TLC, OutKast, Craig Mack, and The Notorious B.I.G., to name a few.

To call it a "dream job" was an understatement. Know this: A "dream job" is HARD WORK! I worked my behind off so that my artists would have the best representation in the press. I put out many fires daily, cranked out copy-worthy press releases, and yes, answered a minimum of 250 calls per day. I never considered how many calls I was receiving until Dickie, the beloved Arista receptionist with all of his eccentricities, quipped, "You receive more calls through this switchboard than any other employee. Hands down!"

I thought, *Mmm ... no wonder I'm so tired!*

There is one call I will never forget, which came from our chieftain, Clive Davis. Peri interrupted the call I was on to advise me that Mr. Davis was on the line. After exchanging pleasantries, he got right down to business, "LaJoyce, from this day forward, I want you to treat Puffy like an artist."

Photo Credit: Elijah (Farmer) Muhammad

Wow, I thought. I needed specific details. "Okay, sir. What do you mean exactly?"

He explained, "I want you to garner press for Puffy just as if he were an artist."

My mind was racing. The cynic in me thought, *Great. Like I need to add one more artist.* The dreamer in me thought, *Great. Okay I am going to put Puffy to work … for real!*

As CEO of Bad Boy Entertainment, Sean "Puffy" Combs (as he was known then) has since come to have many iterations of his name—a publicity nightmare, might I add. Puff (as I called him) was a like a bad little boy always getting in to trouble but he was a creative genius! Every day, and I mean with no exaggeration, EVERY DAY Puffy called to check on the publicity status of his artists or to share a vision he had about something spectacular. He would drop a crazy idea on me and leave it to me to execute. I loved it! Working with his creative genius kept me on my creative toes, and I learned very quickly how to speak "Puffy." With him, there was never a dull moment.

I often joked about his ideas being so outlandish that if he asked me to locate the guy in the news who was scaling New York City skyscrapers and hire him to climb the building at 112 Fifth Avenue so 112 could perform on the building rooftop at 1:12 in the afternoon, I had better find him! Therefore, I did not find Mr. Davis' request odd at all. In fact, when I really thought about it, Puffy was a bona fide star.

Just one week before the request, there was an MTV awards show at Madison Square Garden, and I witnessed how the audience went bananas when Puffy danced onto the stage with the Bad Boy Family of artists. It was not planned at all. He and I had been standing backstage, enjoying the show and nodding to the music, when he spontaneously "Diddy-bopped" across the stage, glistening in an ivory and gold leisure shirt and pants. The audience went WILD. Biggie, Craig Mack, Faith Evans, and Total welcomed him to the stage, making space for him to dance—and dance he did. The girls were screaming like crrrrazyyyy, "Go Puffy! Go Puffy!" I thought to myself, *Now, he's the star.*

When he came off the stage he was out of breath as he hugged me in a moment of exhilaration and half apology for his on-stage spontaneity. "I just couldn't control myself!" he said.

"Don't you dare apologize," I admonished him. "You turned that out and they loved you!" He looked a bit bashful, which surprised me because there was nothing bashful about Puffy. In fact, at one time he was a dancer.

Once my marching orders were received from Mr. Davis, I got to work with Puffy, getting him media trained. I did the best I could within the limited time I had to correct a multitude of his repetitive colloquialisms, which un-nerved me to no end. His favorite was, "You know what I'm saying?" It was his go-to when he did not want to take the time to fully explain himself. To bring it to his attention I always replied, "No, I don't know what you're saying. Puffy, say whatever it is you want to say." I wanted him to understand that by being vague, it would give an interviewer license to fill in the blank. He promised he would work on eliminating that phrase from his lexicon, but to me it seemed like he said it more often than ever. I got the idea to charge him a quarter every time he said "you know what I'm saying."

At first it was a huge joke, and he would hand me dollars after I tallied how many times he said it in one conversation. He was shocked that I would go through the trouble to count it up, but he was more shocked to learn that this bad speech habit was repetitive. I soon moved him from quarters to 50 cents, to one dollar, to five dollars, to 20 dollars! It was soon after the 20-dollar collections he really started saying it less and less. Sometimes, Puffy was a good sport about paying me, and sometimes he did so grudgingly, but I was South-Side-of-Chicago serious about collecting and his improvement.

Before I felt comfortable enough to put him in front of the press for real, I hired our professional media trainer, Dyana Williams, to really help get him ready for prime time with the press.

One of the other things that was a thorn in my side was that he loved to chew a wad of green gum that could be clearly seen while he was talking. It looked awful on television for sure. I would remind him to spit his gum out, or even to hand it over to me. Once backstage at a show I demanded his and Biggie's gum. Being jokesters, they both placed their wads right on my run-of-show sheet!

Although known as a Bad Boy, Puff had an incredibly soft interior that I encouraged him to show every once in a while. One of the things we worked hard to help the public forget was the devastating 1991 Celebrity Basketball event Puffy had hosted at New York's City College. Some eager attendees had started pushing in the line before the doors opened. Sadly, there was a stampede resulting in the death of nine people with 26 being injured. Puffy was devastated by what happened that day.

He would ask me with tears in his eyes, "When will the good I'm doing, like feeding the homeless, and helping underserved kids, be the first thing people ask me?"

I responded from a journalistic point of view, "Unfortunately, this will never go away. But keep doing the good things and eventually they will be on top of your Google search."

I vowed to him I would not allow any journalist to engage in any line of questioning regarding the game tragedy. My promise was tested when one TV broadcaster from WPIX News came to Puffy's office for a day-in-the-life feature. She was one question into the interview when she took a chance to pounce right on the No Discussion list.

Puffy looked at me like a kid who just had his lunch money taken from him. I will never forget how sad his eyes looked, brimming with tears at the very question about the game with cameras rolling. I snatched that microphone right out of the reporter's hand, declaring, "This interview is over!"

As I marched the crew to the elevator, she said softly, "I hope you understand, I had to take my shot."

I was seething! How could she ask him about the game after I told her ass *don't go there!* I needed to measure my words carefully before I responded. "Oh, I understand fully. You took your shot and you lost." In that moment I too fully understood the assignment. Not only was I to

Launching the Notorious V.I.P.

garner publicity, I was to be a gatekeeper and a fierce protector of the Bad Boy Black Genius who called himself "Puffy." Having six brothers, I was crystal clear. Even at the highest level a Black man could attain, there would be someone lurking in the wings to knock him down. Not. On. My. Watch.

Puffy had a strong sense of faith and would pray before every show with his team. At the height of the East Coast/West Coast conflict, we were in Los Angeles for the Soul Train Music Awards and there was a lot of prayer going on among all of us. The tension was noticeably thick, and no one felt the weight of it more than Puffy.

Leaving a rehearsal one evening, I called him over to let him know that he should be extra careful and not to incite any trouble. He said, "Oh, I won't! I'm cool. I'm cool."

I gave him the side eye because I knew he was loaded with Bad Boy antics, so I asked, "Can I pray for you?" He threw up his hands in surrender and I prayed that he would use wisdom and be protected in his comings and goings in hostile territory. "Amen!" he said and hugged me.

The next day at rehearsal, he rushed over to me, "You will not believe we ran in to Tupac and his crew last night!" I'm thinking, *C'mon, Puff! This is LA with its vast terrain, so how in the heck did you "run into" Tupac and his crew?*

He saw the look on my face that screamed *BOY ARE YOU CRAZY?* without saying a word. He explained. "We were getting something to eat, and they were coming when we were leaving. So, we turned around in the street to say 'What's up' to show there are no hard feelings. You know what I'm saying?"

I closed my eyes, shaking my head. "Are you kidding me?"

Smiling and putting his arm around my shoulder, he said, "It was all good. You prayed for me, right?" Before I could say another word, he folded back into the rehearsal. I was in complete disbelief! I counted myself as a prayer warrior indeed but NEVER had I put God to the test to step right in front of the very thing for which I was praying to be protected! That was some Bad Boy foolishness for real.

On that same trip, I had booked *Details* Magazine for a full-length feature and photo spread. When I first made my pitch, the editor wanted to know why Puffy should get the feature. I jokingly answered, "Because he's the Notorious V.I.P." She roared with laughter and booked the interview and photo shoot. Booking Puffy for *Details* was a really BIG deal for him and for me.

Puffy had rented this grand Grecian-style mansion with white columns in the master suite and all throughout the house. There was a glistening swimming pool with an all-white exterior and sparkling blue water. It was the perfect setting.

He was dressed in a crisp ivory linen two piece. The photographer had him lay on the float in the pool with his shirt open with an ivory straw fedora over his face. She took the picture from the balcony of the master bedroom looking down into the pool. It was spectacular!

The *Details* article was all the rage. It painted him in an incredibly positive light. I doubled over laughing because I could NOT believe she ran the headline with my inside joke, "THE NOTORIOUS V.I.P." And just like that ... Sean "Puffy" Combs graduated from being just a Bad Boy to a crossover Star.

Today, I beam with pride at every re-invention of Puff's success. I have fond remembrances of our times together and it brings me joy to know I had a hand in the launch of one of the music industry's brightest Stars ... his personal troubles notwithstanding. *You know what I'm saying?*

Dr. LaJoyce Brookshire is a full-time wife and mother and a part-time everything else. She is a Naturopathic Doctor, a New York Times Bestselling Author, College Professor at and The Clive Davis Institute of Recorded Music at NYU and CUNYs City College campus, and Co-Creator/Co-Founder of Women Behind The Mic. She resides in Pennsylvania with her husband and together they have a young adult daughter who has danced on many prominent stages with the bright lights of global stages in her future.

Launching the Notorious V.I.P.

LaJoyce with Puffy

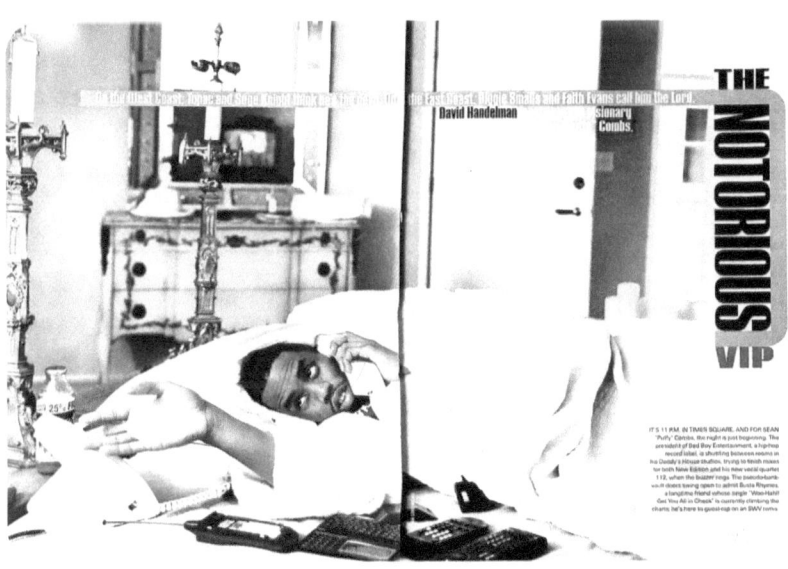

Mic Check 11

"Respect The Architect"
~by~
Michelle Joyce

in·flu·ence *noun*
"The capacity to have an effect on the character, development, or behavior of someone or something, or the effect itself."

I am Michelle Joyce, "MJ," one half of "The LJ and MJ Show," and the Co-Creator and Co-Founder of Women Behind The Mic, The Movement.

On New Year's Eve of 2022, I had an "AHA moment" and realized that on the eve of the 50th anniversary of Hip-Hop, we needed to tell our stories. History is created when it is documented, and I knew that in order to set the record straight, we MUST tell the stories of the women who shaped and shifted a culture. I realized that the stories and features around the men would be told from their perspective and that those stories would not be complete because they were devoid of women. As the legendary writer Harry Allen told me, if you want herstory to be told, you must tell it yourself. That golden nugget was all the motivation that was needed and the journey began.

Needless to say, I came into 2023 HOT.

I did not fall in love with Hip-Hop. I *am* Hip-Hop. I was raised in the BOOGIE DOWN, aka the Bronx, the birthplace of Hip-Hop, and Hip-Hop has been the soundtrack of my life. My childhood best friend LeaNora and I would listen to cassette tapes in her bedroom. The Sugar Hill Gang, Roxanne Shante, Run D-MC, Public Enemy, Salt N Pepa, and Kool Moe Dee were on repeat. When the weather warmed up, LeaNora's big sister and my adopted big sister Leslie would take us to the park jams. Such a vibe! Little did I know at the time that those jam sessions would shape my marketing approach and become the template to break emerging Hip-Hop artists via street and guerilla marketing. I am not new to this, I am true to this.

I've worked in Hip-Hop since the early 1990s and have held entry-level to C-suite positions at The New Music Seminar, EastWest Records, Big Beat, Bad Boy Entertainment, Universal Music, Sony Music, Building Blocks Entertainment, MCA Records, and more. I tell people: "You may not know my name, but you know my work." I have been the marketing engine behind some of the biggest names in music, indie labels, streetwear brands, and corporate initiatives designed to tap into the urban and Hip-Hop market.

I wanted the books that we released during Hip-Hop 50 and beyond to not only tell the stories of the unsung sheroes but to truly reflect their accomplishments and, in a world where women were not celebrated, to give them their long overdue and well-deserved flowers.

As I reflected on the roles that my Sisters played in Hip-Hop, one crucial element stood out to me; and that was that Influencer Marketing was born during the Golden Era of Hip-Hop.

The music industry thought that Hip-Hop was a fad or a fluke. Spoiler. It was not. They had no idea how big it would become or how much it would shape, shift, and create a culture. The powers that be were not aware that Hip-Hop would one day be more than just a genre, that Hip-Hop would become Popular Music and Popular Culture.

Have you ever heard the saying "your network is your net worth"? This holds particularly true in the music industry, which operates like a secret sorority. It's not just about what you know, but who you know. When I landed my first job at EastWest Records, it was no exception. A friend helped me secure an interview, but what really sealed the deal was when my Fairy Godmother, Terri Rossi, who held a senior position at *Billboard* Magazine at the time, personally recommended me to the label head.

I started as the Marketing and Promotion Assistant for the Black music department. While I wasn't new to the music industry, I was new to the label side of things. There was a steep learning curve, which became evident after my first week of training. Yet, when you're truly passionate about something, you're willing to put in the hard work. I made it a point to arrive at the office by 7 a.m., even though our official workday didn't begin until 9 a.m., giving me a two-hour head start on creating the morning reports. One day, I heard someone come in shortly after me. It was none other than the President and CEO, Sylvia Rhone. She asked why I was there so early, and I explained that I was preparing reports to be on my boss's desk by 9 a.m. I often stayed late as well, wanting to tackle as much on my to-do list as possible. Even when you think no one is watching, trust me, they are. My strong work ethic led to a promotion within the first year.

Then, one day, my dear friend Kirk Burrowes visited my office at EastWest Records. I had taken on a new role as the Manager of Rap Promotion and co-founder of W.U.S.U.P. (The WEA Urban Street and University Program). Kirk was working at Orion Pictures at the time and co-founded New York Live, a bi-weekly event featuring music artists. I asked if EastWest could do a showcase with Das EFX and YoYo at the next New York Live event. He took the idea back to the team, and it got a green light. New York Live was a renowned live show event, particularly welcoming to Hip-Hop artists. Fast forward, the event was a massive success. Sylvia Rhone, the President and CEO, attended and witnessed me doing what I do best: Delivering for my artists. Every attendee received an EastWest gift bag filled with promo materials. By the end of the evening, I had generated a buzz that I knew would translate into valuable opportunities.

Kirk visited me a week or two later and told me that he was working with Sean "Puffy" Combs, who was shopping a label deal and when the time was right, he would be coming for me because he really wanted me on his team. My excitement was tempered because in the music industry, talk is just talk until it is not.

In the interim, I interviewed for a job as the Marketing Manager at Big Beat Records and scored the gig. I jumped at the opportunity. I was super excited to work with the R&B duo Changing Faces, the dance diva Robin S., Hip-Hop groups The Artifacts and Down South, and the Queen of Reggae Dawn Penn. I was getting an opportunity to show my marketing genius, as well as a nice pay bump while remaining in the WEA (Warner, Elektra, Atlantic) Family.

But we make plans and God laughs because not even six months into my new gig, my phone rang and it was Kirk asking me if I could meet with Puff that week. No hesitation, *Ummm, YES!!! I sure can! Please name the date and time*! We met at The Shark Bar and were joined by Sybil Pennix, who managed the R&B trio Total, and Kirk. Dinner went well, although I barely ate because … NERVES. I shared my journey to date and the role that I played in breaking Hip-Hop and emerging R&B artists at college and mix-show radio. I got the job! Now the hard part was resigning from Big Beat. Craig Kallman, the label's President, was so gracious, knew how big of an opportunity it was for me. He kindly told me that the door was open if I ever wanted to come back.

The evening that I walked into Bad Boy Entertainment two things occurred: My eyes filled with tears and my life changed in the most beautiful way. I had tears in my eyes because, sitting there on the floor for a team meeting, were all of my new colleagues and all of the faces in that room resembled mine. The team was comprised entirely of people of color and just as it was for me, Hip-Hop was the soundtrack of their lives. I say that my life changed because I was part of a team that launched one of the most successful indie labels of the Golden Era.

I served as the Director of Marketing at Bad Boy Entertainment and worked with a team filled with some of the most incredibly talented women: Kelly Green, Hilary Weston, Leota Blacknor, Cheryl Flowers, LaTrice Shaw, Keisha Dent, Gwen Niles, Glynis Jenkins, Sister Souljah, and others. We embodied the motto "I Am My Sisters Keeper" we had each other's backs like nobody's business.

In my mind, it was not a matter of *if* we would pop. it was simply a matter of when. Sean "Puffy" Combs, the Founder and CEO, was a certified and bona fide Rock Star. He had a successful run at Uptown and a list of hits to his name. Our team was lean and mean and we were hungry. I have always said that I may not be the most intelligent person in the room, but I am the hardest working.

As a brand-new indie label, Bad Boy did not have big budgets so we had to be creative. Our artist roster was comprised entirely of new and developing artists: The Notorious B.I.G., Craig Mack, Total, Faith Evans, and 112. But what we lacked in marketing and promotion budgets we made up with creativity and we had friends who owned or worked for streetwear brands.

I did try reaching out to several mainstream clothing and shoe wear brands but got nowhere. Why? Here's another spoiler: They did not believe that new and developing Hip-Hop and R&B artists had the ability to influence consumers. Yeah. About that ... they were WRONG. Ironically their no became a yes for emerging brands, poetic justice was served.

Today we know that the influence of an influencer is leveraged by brands and marketers to promote their products, services, or messages. In the digital age, brands identify influencers who align with the brand's values, target audience, and demographic. The main objective is to expand and grow your audience organically. Influencers have cultivated their audiences and have earned their trust. But the blueprint was created in the Golden Era.

The Golden Era's Culture Creators knew that if you wanted to reach a young urban consumer, if you wanted to get behind the velvet rope with young Hip-Hop audiences, you needed the co-sign, and that co-sign was a Hip-Hop artist or tastemaker. By dressing our artists for video shoots, press days, photo shoots, and promo tours, etcetera, brands would have the opportunity to tap into a consumer base they were struggling to reach. No bites? No problem. We can show you better than we can tell you. And when we do, you'll be calling.

By the time Craig Mack's single "Flava In Your Ear" went gold, we had brands calling the office. When we released Biggie's single "Juicy," packages from brands started to arrive. And by the time we were in preproduction for the Craig Mack "Flava In Your Ear Remix" video, things had started to reach a fever pitch. Do you remember how Oprah famously said "and *you* win a car, and *you* win a car"? Huge boxes would arrive daily with shoes, sneakers, boots, clothes, jackets, hats. Note to self: We showed you.

Bad Boy Entertainment was known for our innovative and groundbreaking marketing techniques. Our music videos were legendary. When a single dropped, consumers were always waiting for the even more epic remix, and we created the blueprint for collaboration culture to create buzz around our artists and our releases. Collaborations were the point of entry to expand our artists' reach organically. We also set the bar for promotional campaigns. The B.I.G. Mack campaign was shot at a fast-food restaurant in NYC, the "B.I.G. Mack Mixtape" was delivered in a cardboard burger box printed with "B.I.G. Mack" on the top, and the mixtape itself was tucked away in a burger bun.

The "Flava In Your Ear Remix" video was the perfect storm and showcased the genius that was young Puff in the most brilliant way. It highlighted just how we changed the game through the power of key collaborations. The song and video featured Craig Mack, Biggie, LL Cool J, Busta Rhymes, Rampage, and Keisha Spivey from Total. The video was directed by Hype Williams and included cameos by Das EFX, Mic Geronimo, Irv Gotti, and Funkmaster Flex.

Influencer marketing has a Mama, and she was born during the Golden Era of Hip-Hop. As I mentioned earlier, by aligning with Hip-Hop artists, numerous brands were "put on" because our artists were not only trendsetters, they were also cultural icons whose co-sign of these products carried significant weight. Additionally, if you were a brand whose target demo was a young urban youth, then you needed to have a conversation with us, because we (Hip-Hop marketers and brand strategists) were the gatekeepers and Hip-Hop artists were the key. The endorsement of brands by Hip-Hop artists who had genuine credibility had a powerful impact on consumer perception and that translated to sales.

During the Golden Era of Hip-Hop, emerging brands often had limited marketing budgets much like indie labels. By creating strategic partnerships, we found a cost-effective way to dress our artists and the brands had the opportunity to reach a large and engaged audience. We knew the power that Hip-Hop artists had and we knew that they had the ability to shape trends. What they wore became highly sought after, influencing consumer behavior and purchasing decisions.

I remember the first time B.I.G. wore a Coogi sweater. It was, shall we say, unexpected. At the very next industry party I attended, I spotted no less than five men wearing Coogi sweaters. That is the power of influence. Lil Kim wears a green wig, and not less than a week later I see green wigs in the beauty supply store. That illustrates how Hip-Hop influenced where and how consumers spent their money. I know because I have been that consumer. When Queen Latifah released her single "Ladies First," I had to have the sunglasses she was wearing in the video.

The marketing and promotion tools that we had during The Golden Era of Hip-Hop were music videos, photo shoots, press interviews, promo tours, live media appearances, concerts, and public appearances. Each of these presented an opportunity for product placement and our Hip-Hop artists gave brands the opportunity to collaborate, grow their consumer base, and develop a core audience of young urban consumers.

While the platforms have evolved since then with the advent of social media and digital media, the fundamental principles of leveraging people of influence to showcase your brand and influence consumer spending of discretionary income remain consistent between product placement in the Golden Era of Hip-Hop and modern influencer marketing. Both strategies tap into the power of cultural influence and personal endorsement to drive brand awareness and consumer engagement.

Some incredible street fashion brands emerged during the Golden Era of Hip-Hop, and brands made a significant impact on the fashion industry as a whole. Some of those brands were FUBU (For Us, By Us), Karl Kani, Cross Colours, Walker Wear, PNB Nation, Mecca USA, Phat Farm, Baby Phat, Ecko Unlimited, and RocaWear, just to name a few. Their impact challenged traditional fashion norms and what the face of the brand looked like. The street fashion brands emphasized diversity and inclusivity. These brands demonstrated that urban fashion had broad appeal beyond the Hip-Hop community; urban fashion became popular fashion. The ripple effect was felt on a global scale because it influenced high-end and luxury brands to begin incorporating elements of urban style into their collections.

Those brands left a lasting legacy that continues to this day. Their footprint is still visible in contemporary fashion trends and streetwear culture. The foundation that they laid paved the way for the next generation of streetwear brands and designers, and their work is still relevant today.

As Hip-Hop gained mainstream recognition, artists began incorporating high-end designer fashion into their wardrobes. Brands like Versace, Gucci, and Louis Vuitton became synonymous with luxury in Hip-Hop culture. I remember being on set for Biggie's "One More Chance" video shoot and he was wearing Versace shades. Drops mic. The architects of street style fused urban street wear with luxury brands seamlessly. Let's just say that forming strategic partners, securing brands for product placement, and gaining sponsorships for events got easier and easier with each success.

During my time at Bad Boy, I not only found my forever family and tribe, but I also gained invaluable skills. I learned to uncover hidden opportunities within ideas, thrive under pressure, and accomplish monumental tasks in record time—sometimes within literal minutes.

One particularly memorable and amusing lesson was the importance of making things happen by any means necessary. On one occasion, we were scheduled to meet Puff at his apartment for a TV shoot. We had gone the extra mile to have his apartment professionally cleaned the day before. However, upon arrival with the marketing team, we discovered that he had hosted a gathering the previous evening, leaving the place in disarray. I couldn't help but let out the most exasperated sigh imaginable, giving the situation a side eye. With just an hour before the cameras were set to roll, we knew we had to act fast. The marketing department took charge and cleaned up his apartment. While it wasn't officially part of my job description, the decision to tackle the task was a no-brainer, given the critical importance of the exposure.

I am proud to have been one of Hip-Hop's Culture Curators and Creators. I am that Chick.

Today Michelle Joyce is the co-creator and co-founder of Women Behind the Mic, as well as the Chief Experience Officer of Digital Chick Consulting. She works with clients, crafting social and digital marketing and branding campaigns. Her superpower is the ability to make marketing magic. She resides in New Jersey with her husband.

(L to R) LaJoyce Brookshire, Faith Evans, Michelle Joyce
Photo Credit: Brooke Brookshire

(L to R) Notorious B.I.G., Puffy, Craig Mack

Mic Check 12

"Love & Hip-Hop"
~by~
Lynne Poole

Like many little girls growing up in a household full of love and soulful joy, I was exposed to music at an early age. Most days and especially Saturdays (during the *Soul Train* hour) our house was filled with music and I loved singing into a hairbrush, using it as my microphone …IYKYK! As the youngest child of four, I always followed behind my siblings; it was their love of music that helped shape my view. The music and artists during the late '60s and early '70s—Motown, the Isley Brothers, Earth Wind & Fire and Stevie Wonder to name a few—was food for my soul. Of course, I had no idea at the time that my life would forever be changed by this fascinating artform called music.

My Hip-Hop story begins in Cleveland, Ohio, my hometown—now home to the Rock and Roll Hall of Fame. My first time hearing a rap song was during an end-of-school-year backyard party at my best friend JoAnn (Chapman) Pitts' house in the '80s; the song was "Rapper's Delight" by The Sugarhill Gang and it was taking the community by storm. Our minds were blown away by the thumping rhythm and cadence in which they rapped—this was new to us! Remember, Cleveland was not New York City. The DJ must have played that song 20 times that evening and we couldn't get enough of listening to the lyrics that made you want to try recite them in the same manner they were rapping.

Of course, that night no one thought rap music would last …

During my summer breaks from Kent State University, I worked at a record store called Record Rendezvous. It was here that I was introduced to the world of record labels, and I befriended many of the company representatives. When I graduated from college, I obtained a merchandising position at Warner/Elektra/Atlantic Distribution (WEA). Shortly thereafter, Richard Nash, then the local Atlantic Records rep who was being relocated to New York, recommended me to Sylvia Rhone, who was the newly appointed VP of Urban Promotion. She offered me the open radio promotions position. In this position I worked with many artists, visiting radio, retail, and club events in the region, which consisted of Cleveland and Columbus, Ohio; Buffalo and Rochester, New York; and Pittsburgh, Pennsylvania—all major radio markets.

Not only was I in the music business, my brother Ralph Poole was a prominent on-air personality at 93-FM WZAK, a station responsible for exposing Hip-Hop music into the Cleveland and Northeast Ohio marketplace.

As a promo rep, the first two Hip-Hop artists I worked with were up and coming out of Brooklyn, New York: MC Lyte and Audio Two. They were signed to Atlantic Records by way of First Priority Music. I admit, it was so refreshing. Not only were they super talented, they were young and intelligent about life, music, and world events. Having worked mainly R&B records, I found that this new genre of music opened a whole new world for me in my position. I now started working with the mix show DJs, going to younger/hipper clubs, even wearing different clothes. One thing I learned early on working with Hip-Hop artists was the connection young people would have to the music and the influence the artist could weld because of it, so I always made sure to incorporate school and community center visits, allowing for one-on-one contact between the two.

I have to recognize Sylvia Rhone and Atlantic Records for being the first major label to commit to this new up-and-coming artform that would go on to become one of the most successful genres in music. In fact, Atlantic signed a single deal early on with an unknown rapper from Brooklyn by the name of Jay-Z, who today is the most influential Hip-Hop artist of all time.

One of Atlantic's independent label partnerships was with Ruthless Records, at the time under the leadership of Eric "Eazy-E" Wright. Among the artists who would emerge from this deal was a Dallas-based rapper by the name of The D.O.C., whose debut album *No One Can Do It Better* was produced by Dr. Dre. When I say he burst onto the scene with a vengeance...! His song "It's Funky Enough" with dope lyrics "One, and here comes the two to the three and four then I drop the beat I have in store..." and a wicked, undeniable beat, raced up the charts, becoming the fastest gold-selling rap song at the time. I was so proud of the success we had with this project and couldn't wait to see what would come next for this uber-talented individual. Unfortunately, his career was later sidelined by a car accident that damaged his vocal cords.

Around this same time (1989), Sylvia Rhone was making changes in the NY market and asked if I would be interested in moving to New York City. I accepted the opportunity and never looked back. My introduction to the New York/Eastern regional music market—which included Boston—was swift. This new challenge was eye opening and I loved the fast pace of the city. The NYC radio stations KISS-FM and WBLS were powerhouses and it was tough getting records added, but in time I fit right in. The popular mix show/rap DJs at this time were Red Alert at KISS and Chuck Chillout at WBLS and eventually I developed great working relationships with both.

I also have to give major props to DJ Clark Kent, who was in our A&R department responsible for signing new artists. He was a popular New York club DJ and he would often lend his help in connecting me to the rap DJs in the market.

Over the years, while still in the promotions position, I was fortunate to have many great experiences working with Hip-Hop artists, and the team at Atlantic would work with some of the best. In fact, LeVert's single "Just Coolin'" was one of the first R&B singles to feature a Hip-Hop artist on the hook—none other than Heavy D!

In the early 1990s, my Hip-Hop story took a personal turn when I met, dated, and married Keith Shocklee, the legendary producer, founding member of Public Enemy, and now Rock and Roll Hall of Fame Inductee. In addition to PE, he and his brother Hank, together known as The Bomb Squad, produced some of rap's biggest projects: LL Cool J, Ice Cube, and the movie soundtracks to *Do The Right Thing* ("Fight the Power") and *Juice*, to name a few. Chuck D and Flavor Flav were in our wedding—and yes, Flav wore a clock that matched his tuxedo. I guess I was *Love and Hip-Hop* before *Love and Hip-Hop*… full stop!

While still at Atlantic Records, I was promoted to the sales department where very few Blacks or women worked, eventually overseeing the urban sales across the country; in this capacity, I helped market the debut release of Lil' Kim's Hardcore project with the Untertainment Records team. This project had the entire music industry abuzz—Lil' Kim, her infamous squatting cover art and hit singles were on fire.

Following my stint at Atlantic Records, I was hired by Epic Records as Senior Director of Urban Sales. Upon my new association with Epic, some of the first Hip-Hop projects I helped develop sales and marketing plans for were Camron, DJ Envy, Ghostface Killah, DJ Kay Slay, and Jennifer Lopez's singles featuring LL Cool J and Ja Rule.

Over the next few years, I served in various capacities at Sony Music Entertainment, where I was able to be at the forefront of working with the promotions, sales, and product management teams to create and execute plans for new and established Hip-Hop artists.

I feel very proud to be a part of the foundation and development of what Hip-Hop has become today: one of the leading artforms in the world as well as recognized in the Rock and Rock Hall of Fame. Hip-Hop has always been Bold, Defining, Transformative, Informational and Trendsetting…it was only waiting for the rest of the world to catch up.

Today Lynne Poole is working in government, living in the Long Island, New York, area. She enjoys spending time with family and close friends. She is active in her church and community where was recently appointed to the Westbury Arts Council Board of Directors.

Lynne with Lil' Kim's Platinum placque

(L to R) Lynne, Wendy Williams, MC Lyte

Mic Check 13

"Taking My Shot"
~by~
Lynn M. Scott

"Lynn, you need a job!" my mom and Nana said.

"I've been looking," I answered with my Scorpio sassiness. I was on my gap year (at the time I didn't know what that was, all I know is my mom didn't have a college fund waiting for me when I graduated high school). But right there in the newspaper, I found an advertisement for an internship at a music label not far from Queens Boulevard. I walked into the interview armed with only my confidence and a desire to get a summer job.

I didn't have a clue that I was walking into my destiny. God did.

I interviewed with Michael Weiss. I don't remember much about the interview except that it was non-paying and that he asked me what radio station I listened to. I told him I listened to Frankie Crocker on WBLS and I also told him that I wouldn't work for free. I must have said something right because I got the job. This was my first employment negotiation where I advocated for myself, and it worked out in my favor.

Destiny.

I learned a lot while at Sam and Nervous Records. I worked with club DJs, radio program directors, label executives, managers, agents, and a warehouse full of people who pressed physical products: vinyl records, CDs, and promotional items. It was a great introduction to the music business.

Photo Credit: @MacThaShooter

I left Sam Records with experience, a little money, and confidence in tow.

Next stop on my Book Of Life tour was North Carolina A&T State University. I was a NYC student on a mission to be a corporate litigation attorney. That was what I thought and planned…but God!

Enter Shakim Compere, the acclaimed and accomplished manager of multi-hyphenate Queen Latifah and the steward of Flavor Unit Management. I met Shakim when Latifah came to A&T to perform at Corbett Sports Center. My homegirl Swatch was dancing for her so I was able to get up close and personal to both Sha and La while they were in Greensboro, North Carolina. Somehow through that encounter, Shakim was impressed by me and later came looking for me to join the Flavor Unit team in East Orange, New Jersey, as the receptionist. I contemplated the offer and decided to make the leap, leave college, and join the team. That decision changed the trajectory of my life. I started as the receptionist and within three years, I was the General Manager and VP of Artist Development. I became a pretty accomplished young Black woman who left college to pursue a career in music within three short years. It turned out to be a great chapter in my personal Book Of Life.

While at Flavor Unit, I worked very closely with Queen Latifah, Naughty By Nature, Black Sheep, Zhané, and a young trio named The Fu-Schnickens, among others.

While in my office, the receptionist transferred a call from an arrogant man. By this time, on our incredible journey, we were in our firehouse at 155 Morgan Street. We had beautiful offices with no ceilings on the first floor. Back to the rude-ass man that called.

I said, "Flavor Unit Management, this is Lynn."

"Hello, this is…" let's call him an "agent," "calling regarding Shaquille O'Neal."

I responded "Who?" and "What is a Sha kill oh kneel?"

"You don't know who Shaquille O'Neal is?"

I responded, "No."

He was amazed that I had no clue and said, "He's going to be the first-round draft pick for the upcoming NBA draft." Clearly, I needed to get up to speed on sports. He shared that his client was a big fan of the Fu-Schnickens. I mentioned it in the office and it seemed this was pop culture news I needed to know. I then called the guys to tell them about the talented basketball player about to turn pro who was a big fan of theirs. They were very, very excited and were open to doing whatever Shaquille wanted to do.

Fast forward a couple of months. Shaquille O'Neal dropped 16 bars on their song "Tru Fuschnick" and actually became the first-round draft pick for the 1992 NBA Draft. Shaquille began calling himself Shaq-Fu with the success of the remix. He was so inspired by the experience and success that he signed a record deal with Jive Records to record his own album. Of course, he invited the Fu-Schnickens to feature on his first single, "What's Up Doc? (Can We Rock?)" and Shaquille was on his way to platinum album success. He took rapping, and his music career, very seriously. His work ethic was impressive.

While I was at Flavor Unit and we were working together, I didn't realize that Shaq was watching how I moved, worked, and supported my artists. His agent asked me to join his team. I didn't want to join his agent's team but I was intrigued by the intersection of music, sports, and branding. At the time I didn't articulate it that way, but I knew deeply that the collaboration of these worlds was interesting and very new.

I was tormented. I spent months struggling with the idea of leaving Flavor Unit and partnering with Dennis Scott from the Orlando Magic to manage Shaquille O'Neal—the world's most popular basketball player due to his dunk spectacles and free throws. The thoughts that swirled in my head were deafening. Was I ready? Could I actually be successful on my own without Shakim? Could I make a difference in Shaquille's musical career? Was I qualified? Would I be respected? Is leaving a good idea? Do I have what it takes?

I eventually made the decision to leave Flavor Unit and move to Orlando to work with Shaq.

I learned that I was armed with exactly what I needed to support Shaquille in his music endeavors. We were very successful with his first two albums, 1993's *Shaq Diesel* (platinum) and 1994's *Shaq Fu: Da Return* (gold), and the singles "I Know I Got Skillz" (gold) and

"What's Up Doc (Can We Rock?)" (gold). These were his only successful RIAA-certified releases.

While working with Shaq, I saw that he approached everything with dedication and professionalism. He had something to prove on the court and behind the mic. He balanced it all like Superman. He did promo, filmed videos, signed his very own Reebok sneakers that we bundled with physical product, appeared at music awards shows, and did everything in between. Working in collaboration with the Jive team, we made Shaquille a bona fide rap star, shedding all novelty perception.

Unbeknownst to me, however, while in the midst of doing what I do, I was facing challenges from within the internal camp. I couldn't see it because I have always been the executive that puts her head down and does the work. This all came to a head while we were gathered at Shaquille's beautiful home in the suburbs of Orlando. I got a clue while meeting in the kitchen, though I can't quite remember the details of the meeting. I do remember that I felt small.

The agent and I were not aligned. He made it a point to tell me that I was using my proximity to Shaquille to advance my career. He said it in a way to demean me and make it appear to Shaquille that I was ineffective. I made it very clear to him that while Shaquille was a big deal in the NBA, he didn't have the same impact in music. We had to build it. Establish the respect that Shaquille wanted. I found myself being defensive and completely shattered by the pushback from the suits who had no clue what to do with his rap career. I walked out of the kitchen and into the great room.

I was followed into the room by Shaq's mom, Miss Lucille. She encouraged me and said empowering words to get me back in the game and in full support of her son. She said, and I'm paraphrasing, "I see that you care for my son, and you know what you're doing, don't let them push you out, stay strong."

I remained on Shaquille's team for his first two albums and the associated singles yielding platinum and gold status. Shaquille fired me before releasing his third album. I was never one to tell him "yes" unless the "yes" was the right answer for the situation. As a result, I found myself out. It was a great ride and I'm forever grateful for the experience of leading and working with so many incredible people, especially Leah Wilcox and Chrysa Chin, who were constant reminders that I could hang with the boys and win.

After separating from Shaquille, I made the decision to learn more about pop acts. I worked briefly at Transcontinental (home to Backstreet Boys, N'Sync, and Britney Spears). Working under executive Johnny Wright turned out to be a gift that would pay in dividends later when I worked at Universal Music Group and beyond. I have had the honor to work with some of the greatest artists/entertainers of all time: Queen Latifah, Beyoncé, Jay-Z, Erykah Badu, Enrique Iglesias, Jennifer Lopez, Nelly, Kelly Rowland, Prince, and Duran Duran, to name just a few.

Every experience that I encountered built me into the student leader that I am today. Throughout my career, I have never wavered in my commitment to the artists I worked with, the art they create, the culture they contribute to, and the audiences who power it all. I'm still leading and learning as the VP, Label Services and Client Success, for a successful and growing music tech company.

Today, Lynn M. Scott is the VP, Vydia Label Services and Client Success. Vydia provides an end-to-end solution to empower the next generation of music creators, managers, and labels. She enjoys working with a myriad artists from developing to superstar. Lynn is currently living in Los Angeles and is the proud mom of three adult children. In her spare time, she loves to hike, travel, experience cultural cuisine, attend California Worship Center, and watch Netflix and chill with her family. She wakes up daily with a grateful heart, a curious mind, and a passionate heart with a desire to make a difference in her pursuit to help and protect artists.

Lynn with Shaquille O'Neal

Mic Check 14

"The Great Executive Expectation"
~by~
Stone Love Fauré

My time working in the music industry in the 1990s remains one of the most formative experiences of my life. I was fresh out of San Francisco State University, majoring in Broadcast Communication, in my mid-20s. I jumped at the unexpected opportunity presented to me by my dear friend, Kymberlee Thorton, who was a well-established record executive. She included me in her close circle of professionals, to join the marketing team at Bust It/Capital Records. After my internships at RCA and Motown, I was eager to roll up my sleeves and make a real impact at a label like Capital/Bust It Records. Little did I know then how this job would shape my early career and open my eyes to the realities behind the music business fantasy.

I joined Bust It just as MC Hammer was taking off; I was thrown into the whirlwind of promoting a bona fide superstar. The first surprise was how tedious and grunt-heavy much of the daily work was. At RCA, I'd spent more time packing boxes with products to adoring fans than hobnobbing with artists. The glamorous image of industry parties and concerts was just an illusion. Still, I was determined to soak up every learning experience.

My role was focused heavily on radio promotion and marketing to record stores in a specific region. From the outside, radio seemed like an exciting tastemaker bringing new music to eager fans. Although

Photo Credit: Lindsay Miller Photography

Hammer legitimately eared his title as the Number One entertainer in the world, a sad reality was that music we consumed was a calculated game of payola and politics. The record companied carried favor with program directors. They decided which company's artist got airplay. Talent didn't guarantee success—you had to lobby and leverage relationships. I was disappointed to learn the songs I heard were more about back-room deals than quality.

The upside was representing a quality product and traveling in style with Hammer's team as his fame exploded. We were treated like VIPs everywhere we went, whether posh restaurants or packed arenas. My kids loved getting caught up in the Hammer-mania, basking in the spotlight-by-association at school. For a young mom, it was a thrill to jet around the country and get the celebrity treatment.

Not everything behind the scenes was glamorous, though. I was taken aback by the boys' club culture and how crass everyday language could be. At one heated sales meeting, a manager referred to me derogatorily as a "bitch." Naively hoping to clear the air, I later asked him politely not to use that term. He exploded; hurling expletives to make clear I was not his "woman." Therefore, he could speak to me as he pleased. After instinctively defending myself, I was suspended three days.

That intense exchange was a wake-up call, forcing me to reflect. I realized I needed to be in a more professional environment or risk sinking to that level. Music could bring out my demons if I didn't establish personal boundaries. None of the vulgarity or politics changed how hard I worked, though. When challenges arose, the team came together.

Our biggest test was an all-out marketing blitz to dethrone Michael Jackson's chart-topping album *Thriller*. We wanted the impossible: to beat the King of Pop himself. After months of grueling promotion of *Please Hammer Don't Hurt 'Em*, we did the unthinkable: Hammer's album hit Number One for a record-shattering 29 consecutive weeks—eight more than MJ! On the day the news broke, that same abrasive manager picked me up in a bear hug and said, "You're a hell of a woman." Shared joy erased past divides.

Looking back, I'm proudest of our *Billboard* achievement, earning Hammer a diamond certification, platinum certification, and countless other awards from Billboard, Top Black Charts, and Capital Records. But my deepest rewards were intangible: growth, relationships, lessons about integrity. I learned to take the good with the bad and not lose myself in the process. When everything was new and exciting, I was able to pace myself and make transitions seem easy. When touring got lonely or chauvinism surfaced, it tested my resilience and I persevered through it all.

Through ups and downs, I loved witnessing the behind-the-scenes process of building an icon. Watching Hammer, a musician and a record label mogul I worked with daily, become a cultural sensation was unreal. I gained much respect for the executive and management team at Bust It.

Hammer was everywhere almost overnight—on TV, magazines, live tours, and radio. Literally, Hammer mastered every medium.

No matter how many records I later worked on, that rush was once-in-a-lifetime.

My time as an executive in music shaped me as a marketer and as a person. I learned the importance of relationships in any collaborative field like radio. Challenging work environments forced me to define my values. Travel opened my horizons and worldview. I saw how image and marketing converged to create larger-than-life stars, manufacturing the illusion teens, young adults and mature audiences idolized.

Witnessing the unglamorous grind behind Hammer's meteoric rise was eye opening. I had to grow a thicker skin to flourish in the testosterone-fueled energy of labels in those days. Most of all, I learned to take joy in accomplishments without losing myself. When you love the work, even setbacks have silver linings. For all its ups and downs, I'm grateful I got to live out my music industry dream. Those years made me wiser in my career and life,

...And that, you can't touch.

Today, Dr. Stone Love Fauré is a highly accomplished motivational speaker, essayist, personal coach, and faith-powered global seminar presenter. With a deep commitment to transformative healing and a profound understanding of the decision-making process, she stands at the intersection of lived experience and deep inquiry. As the author of Decision Time: How Strength Based Decision Making Changes Everything *(2015), Dr. Stone Love provides readers with a comprehensive step-by-step process for making optimal decisions in every situation. In the memoir, "Now, I Am Her: The Woman I've Always Been, But Had Never Known," she shares her own journey of vulnerability, growth, and self-discovery. Driven by her mission to empower individuals, she has garnered recognition and acclaim on a worldwide scale.*

Stone Love's with MC Hammer plaque

# Mic Check 15

"Presenting Crazy Sexy Cool TLC"
~by~
Carin Thomas

I was a junior in college in 1983 when I learned the system for sneaking into Contempo's Nightclub in Los Angeles on Sunday nights. I was only 20. I didn't have a fake ID, but the game was pretty simple.

Contempo's opened at 9 p.m., but no one was in the front to check IDs and collect the cover charge prior to 9, so my girls and I would get in free around 8:30, buy a Coke at the bar, take a seat, and wait for the amazing Louil Silas, Jr., to start the dance party with Howard Johnson's song.

So fine. Blow my mind. Ooh…

And the crack of that sound system blew my mind!

It was on the dance floor that I met KABC morning talk show air personality Russ Parr. I'll never forget our conversation, yelling back and forth over the music. Russ said he had graduated from the same college I attended and had chosen the same major: Cal State University, Northridge—Radio, TV, and Film.

I knew he was full of it. I called him a liar.

Then he shouted out my professors. It was hilarious!

So, Russ Parr became my first mentor in a near 20-year career.

He later joined the morning show at AM Stereo-KDAY, where Hip-Hop was introduced to the airwaves in Los Angeles. He called me to offer an interview because the Program Director needed an assistant. I declined because I was still a full-time senior. But after I graduated, Russ called again. It was September of 1985, my birthday month. That same KDAY Program Director, Jack Patterson, needed another assistant, and that time I accepted an interview. I got the job after answering "yes" to one key question.

"Can you write and spell? I need to be able to ask you to 'handle it'."

At the station, every Monday was "Music Day." The record label promoters would come to see the Music Director, Gregg Mack, to peddle their music for airplay. Every Monday, these swaggadelic brothers and sisters rolled up in Beemers and Benzes with their records and concert tickets. (I drove a Datsun B2-10.) On any given day, they would also bring their artists for on-air interviews. And because I was the assistant to the Program Director, they often went through me. Talk about networking!

Fast forward to 1989…

I had been Promotions Assistant, and then Traffic Manager at KDAY. I had my sights on Music Director, but Jack wouldn't give me the job—and I knew why. New music, aka "gangster rap," emerged from key players in L.A.'s gang culture. So, instead of hiring me, Jack hired Steve Washington from Tower Records. I was disappointed, but the message was clear.

Steve was over 6 feet tall. He was yoked like Mr. Universe and his handshake was freakin' painful. I was a lanky little ballet dancer, fresh out of college. Jack didn't want to expose me to the gang element, so he protected me by hiring Steve.

I'm still grateful for not getting that job.

So, it was time to go. I had outgrown KDAY. Being on the frontline of that cool lifestyle made me look at those label promotors and wonder, "How much money are they making? I can do that!" I then contacted every record promotor in town in hopes of getting a label job.

Ken Wilson from Columbia Records introduced me to his new National Director, Barbara Lewis who needed an assistant, so on Ken's word, she hired me. When Barbara took the position of VP of Black Music at Capitol Records, Ken replaced her at Columbia, and I continued my mentorship under him. (Ken taught me to read everything I came across—even if it was none of my business!) Months later, Barbara brought me over to Capitol and gave me the Regional Promotions Manager position.

I was really in the game, but there was nothing flossy about it. Promoting records was emotional and stressful—but at times, super fun. Technology was the rage: Beepers. Cell phones. Blackberries. Multitasking never stopped. The message was: Be everywhere. Don't miss an opportunity to expose your product—and don't miss an opportunity to create opportunities where there aren't any.

Then I'd hear Russ's voice in my head: *"Pressure is something you put on yourself."*

So, I powered through and eventually landed promotions positions at Arista Records (including the LaFace, Bad Boy, and Rowdy labels), Universal, and Warner Brothers Records.

I don't remember when I fell in love with Hip-Hop. I was a global music lover, so I didn't identify Hip-Hop as a "thing"—only as a spoken-word extension of R&B. I've always believed the words of Quincy Jones: *"There are only two types of music. Good and bad."*

And much of what they were calling Hip-Hop was good. Real good. It didn't matter that the artists weren't singers. The beats, the samples, and the crafty storytelling were addictive. Rap music and Hip-Hop flavor turned gifted, articulate, artsy black youth into neighborhood superstars!

There were so many experiences, but one that was most memorable and rewarding centered on launching the girl group TLC.

In 1992, I was a Regional Promotions Manager at Arista/LaFace, and was responsible for getting TLC's debut single "Ain't Too Proud To Beg" on the radio. This was LaFace's first female group, and a lot was riding on their success. At the time, Los Angeles was the number one sales market in the country, and the competition was insane. Mary J. Blige, Bel Biv DeVoe, and a gazillion Teddy Riley productions dominated the airwaves and there I was, a wannabe influencer, trying to get TLC "added" at the heavyweight R&B station KKBT 92.3 The Beat.

But the Program Director, Mike Stradford, wouldn't add the song right away. He thought "Ain't Too Proud To Beg" sounded okay, but the record had to prove itself. He wanted to wait and see if it caught on in other markets.

On Music Day, I couldn't just continue to talk about airplay and sales in other markets. I needed an angle, so I called on Danny "Fut" James, Director of Impact Record Pool, for help at the club level. He distributed new music every Saturday and agreed to survey his DJ members and get feedback on TLC directly from the dancefloor. Meanwhile, our street teams had been distributing promo copies of TLC throughout the West Coast, and the video was in rotation.

Nice. Whatever…

The following Saturday, Fut handed me 75 DJ surveys that evidenced inquiries and requests for "Ain't Too Proud To Beg." I made two sets of copies. One set for my files and one for my boss in New York City. The following Music Day, I delivered the originals to The Beat, and after seeing the feedback, Mike agreed to play the song.

And Mikey liked it! It sounded good on the radio. And then he officially added it to the playlist.

After that, "Ain't Too Proud To Beg" blew up and set the stage for the second single, "Baby, Baby, Baby," that became a Number One song on *Billboard*'s Hot R&B/Hip-Hop Singles chart. TLC's debut album, *Oooooooohhh on the TLC Tip*, quickly sold one million copies and was eventually certified a four-times-Platinum seller.

Relationships drove the work. Everything else was icing. By using local data, I leveraged my relationship with Impact Record Pool to influence the decision-maker at KKBT.

No one taught me how to do that—and to my knowledge, none of the local music reps used the record pool's resources that way. Surveying DJs was Fut's idea, which came out of a "How am I gonna get this record played?" gripe session. It was worth a shot—and it worked.

To date, TLC is part of an elite class of recording artists with RIAA Diamond Certifications. Diamond equates to ten million records sold. Worldwide, TLC has sold more than 65 million records!

65+ Million!

Few words can describe how I feel about the world celebrating 50 years of Hip-Hop Culture—50 years of Our Culture. It is surreal to have witnessed the way music, art, and style, in all of its beautiful blackness, permeated the general market and validated our stories.

Pride and gratitude are my biggest takeaways, for it was The Culture that shaped my entire adult life. I am one of the lucky ones—lucky to have been in the right place, at the right time, among the right people.

Many of our pioneering souls are no longer here to celebrate this milestone anniversary. We are the beneficiaries and the carriers of their vision. May they rest in power, but The Culture must never rest. Fifty years marks the beginning of Hip-Hop's forever.

Our forever.

So fine. Blow my mind. Oooooooohhh…

Carin Thomas

Carin Thomas is an Education Administrator in the Special Education Division of the New York City Department of Education. She serves as an instructional/behavioral coach in Brooklyn and offers professional development to school administrators and teachers of students with disabilities. Carin loves ballet and grew up dancing in Los Angeles. She also enjoys artmaking, flower design, painting, food, and photography. She is married to a former record label executive and currently resides in New Jersey.

Carin with TLC in Las Vegas

Carin with TLC in Los Angeles, California

Mic Check 16

"Find Your Passion"

~by~

Tracey J. Jordan

*Find your passion and you'll find your road to success.
When you love what you do, it's no longer work, it's passion!*

I was born and raised in New York City. My mom is N.E.A. Jazz Master Sheila Jordan, and my father, the late Duke "Jordu" Jordan, was a jazz pianist for, among others, saxophone great Charlie Parker. I was born with music in my genes, but not in a musical sense. I don't sing or play an instrument, which is always embarrassing when you're the offspring of musicians. You're always asked, "So, what do you play?" I usually snap back with, "The computer."

I attended the High School of the Performing Arts as a theater major. I loved theater and, as a teen, studied acting with the late Herbert Berghof and Uta Hagen at H.B. Studios. I was also awarded a scholarship as a junior member of Arthur Mitchell's Dance Theatre of Harlem. After graduating high school, I moved to Norway and London for two years. In Scandinavia, I started modeling, which was

Photo Credit: @MaroHagopian

easy. Besides a few transplanted jazz musicians like my father, I was one of only a few African-American women living there. Then I moved back to the States and wasn't such a rarity anymore. As a bi-racial model back then, I had difficulty landing commercial gigs, and at 5'8", I wasn't tall enough to do runway shows. I got a few gigs and worked in Ralph Lauren's showroom. But into my early 20s, I realized I wouldn't grow any taller and wasn't getting any cuter, so I better find another career goal unless I wanted to do retail sales.

I called my good friend Katie Valk, a publicist for the P.R. firm Solters Roskin Friedman (S.R.F.). They handled all the heavyweights of the day, Sinatra, Streisand, Parton, Tony Bennett, Berry Gordy/Motown Records, Ron Delsener's Concerts on the Pier and Jones Beach, and all the critical shows on Broadway. Katie Valk and Diana Parker ran the music department, and when they offered me the job as their assistant, I jumped in head first! I taught myself how to type in a matter of days. As for writing? Well, that took considerably longer, but I couldn't have been in a better circumstance to learn. Some of the best P.R. writers in the business worked at S.R.F., and I was lucky to learn from them. You could say S.R.F. was where I earned my degree in public relations!

The position at S.R.F. launched my music, television, and film publicist career. I fell in love with P.R. It was instant gratification when I landed an artist on a magazine cover, a feature interview, a T.V. appearance, an album or concert review, or an item on Page Six, Cindy Adams, or Liz Smith's column! I tagged with Katie and Diana when one of them booked on Live at Five, G.M.A., The Today Show, David Letterman, photo sessions, and radio interviews. I read everything that passed under my nose and became a sponge for learning everything about P.R. I had found my passion and created a niche for myself at S.R.F., handling their R&B projects like Motown Records, Motown Returns to the Apollo, Berry Gordy's *The Last Dragon*, Berry

Gordy, Smokey Robinson, Vanity, Irene Cara, Harry Belefonte's *Beat Street*, *Breakin'* and Morris Day in *Purple Rain*, amongst others. I remained at S.R.F. for five years, which gave me the time and experience to grow into a senior publicist with an excellent reputation. My name was out there, and then, an incredible opportunity knocked.

My first position at a recording label was at renowned music executive Clive Davis's Arista Records. Through Melani Rogers and Abby Konowitch, I secured the Director of R&B Artist Development & Publicity position. It was a fantastic place to work, and Clive Davis would not only become a mentor but, to this day, one of my forever friends. It was Clive who talked me out of going to an acting audition for Bill Cosby for a movie role he offered me. Clive never explained why auditioning for Cosby was a bad idea; he just said, "Don't do it," and that was enough for me!

At Arista Records, I started a lifelong friendship with the Queen of Soul, Ms. Aretha Franklin. Aretha was not traveling outside Detroit then, so I spent much time there. It reached the point whereby she had me stay at her house in an upstairs bedroom next door to her sister Carolyn. Carolyn Franklin and I got on like a house on fire; she was hilarious but always getting us into trouble with Aretha! One night we were drinking beer and smoking in her room. We opened the window and set off the silent alarm that was only audible in Aretha's bedroom downstairs. Needless to say, I was not invited to stay at the house anymore; it was hotels for me! I worked with some of the most talented artists and music executives in the business at Arista, including Whitney Houston, Dionne Warwick, Whodini, Billy Ocean, Kenny G, Exposé, Taylor Dayne, Jermaine Jackson, Gil Scott-Heron, and on the executive side; Don Ienner, Melani Rogers, Lynn Volkman, Tony Anderson, Roy Lott, Monte Lipman, Ken Levy, Doug Daniel, Eliza Brownjohn, and Jim Cawley, amongst many others. I worked at Arista Records for an incredible five years.

At the tail end of my tenure at Arista, I got two simultaneous job offers, one from Ruben Rodriguez at Columbia Records and one from Jheryl Busby, who had just taken over the reins at Motown Records with Berry Gordy's blessing. Both offers were the same money and position, Senior Director, Artist Development & Publicity, and I was torn. The job with Busby meant moving to Los Angeles, and as a native New Yorker living in Manhattan, I had never learned how to drive. The position with Rodriguez was in Columbia's Black Rock building on Sixth Avenue and 51st Street, a much easier commute.

My forever friend Monica Lynch, President of Tommy Boy Records at the time, gave me the best advice, "Ask both of them to make you a Vice President, and see who comes back with a yes." So, I did, and Jheryl Busby said yes, and I became Vice President of Artist Development of Video of Motown Records. My good friend Nelson George quickly pointed out that I was the first African-American to oversee video production at an American recording label. Like Clive Davis, Jheryl Busby became my mentor and another forever friend. He also introduced me to my next set of mentors, Martha Crowninshield of Boston Ventures and the late great Clarence Avant, who would oversee and spearhead my career for the next 15 years. Another five years passed, and I moved back to New York to become MTV Networks' first African-American Vice-President of Music Talent Development and Video Programming for the music video-based network.

During my tenure at MTV Networks, I worked with the head of programming, Andy Schoen on the creation of MTV Jams. I saw a young comedian on Def Comedy Jam named Bill Bellamy, he did a routine called "The Booty Call," which was brilliant. I contacted my pal Bob Sumner at Def Jam about him and he looped me in with his manager. That same night I went to a Broadway play, and Bill Bellamy was sitting in the seat right in front of me, the rest is MTV history.

Find Your Passion

Bill became the first host of MTV Jams and is a close friend to this day. At MTV I also had to work with the network's Standards and Practices VP. Remember all the blurred videos and audio drops? I was the executive who oversaw video submissions for Bad Boy Records and Death Row Records, so you can well imagine how much fun that was! I worked closely with Puffy, Biggie, Craig Mack, Jimmy Iovine, Suge Knight, Dr. DRE, and Snoop Dogg.

It was the summer of 1993 and I had booked Dr. Dre and Snoop Dogg as co-presenters for the MTV Awards. When they arrived, Snoop was nervous and asked me if there was a quiet place he could hang out after he and Dre presented. I sat Dre and Suge in their seats and put Snoop into the trailer for Christian Slater, as he wasn't scheduled to arrive until the latter part of the show. I got Snoop KFC, his Converse swag bag, and some video games and he was all tucked in, or so I thought. I was standing on the side of the stage getting Janet Jackson and her dancers ready for her performance when I received a call from the show's director Joel Gallen. Joel informed me the Sheriff and the LAPD were there and looking to arrest Snoop. I jumped into immediate publicist mode because I not only wanted to protect my Snoop, but didn't want the *Los Angeles Times* headlines to read, "Snoop Doggy Dogg Arrested Backstage at the MTV Awards."

I ran into the audience and grabbed Suge, who quickly ran off to get his hydraulic convertible Cadillac. Suge met me in front of the trailer, I opened the trailer door and the smoke billowed out like in a Cheech and Chong movie. I yelled at Snoop that the LAPD were looking to arrest him and we gathered up all his belongings. I threw the bag of Converse swag over my shoulder and into the back seat of the car and he and Suge drove off bouncing up and down and out the backstage driveway.

When I got back to my hotel I ran into Redman and his dog Daddy, who would later become a "doggie star" in his own right on Cesar Millan's TV show "The Dog Whisperer." I got to my room and turned on the news to find out Snoop had turned himself in to the LAPD on suspicion of possible murder changes, of which he was later cleared.

Years later I read Snoop's book and he talked about the incident and explained that was his first big break on MTV and there was no way he was going to miss it. Snoop and I are forever friends and often talk about that "fateful day" and how it could have changed his life forever. I love you, Snoopy!

The following year, Jheryl Busby and Martha Crowninshield approached me about becoming a partner and the S.V.P. for a venture idea I had proposed to them years before. It was a Motown Records-themed restaurant chain. The venture was fully funded, and I departed MTV to try my luck in this new world. I didn't have anything to do with the food. I worked alongside the architect, Jay Haverson, on the creative buildout of the restaurants, the look, the memorabilia collection, and their display, securing celebrity investors and merchandise creation. I reached back to my Motown family and tapped my good pal Karen Sherlock to work with me. My partners Brian Daneman and Larry Fish were from Planet Hollywood and oversaw the theme restaurant part of the venture. Greg Saltzman and Jojo Pada handled the P.R. We opened Motown Café locations in New York, Las Vegas, and Orlando, Florida. I also worked on one for a Japanese investment company. Unfortunately, the bottom was about to drop out of the theme restaurant business, and the venture did not continue. I learned so much during my time working with my Motown Café Family! But, to be honest, I thought the music business was cutthroat. The restaurant business is just as bad, if not worse!

Throughout my career, I've played an instrumental role in developing, promoting, exposing, and re-exposing such icons as Aretha Franklin, Diana Ross, Whitney Houston, the Rolling Stones, Stevie Wonder, Snoop Dogg, Dr. Dre, 2-Pac, Warren G, The Dogg Pound,

The Wu-Tang Clan, LL Cool J, Run DMC, Puff Daddy … Diddy … Love, and Notorious B.I.G., to name just a few.

Most recently, I served as Senior Director of Talent & Industry Relations for SiriusXM + Pandora, overseeing the day-to-day talent booking and development for SiriusXM's urban contemporary, urban A.C., urban classic, hip hop, urban talk, jazz, gospel, Latin, and Studio 54 channels. In that capacity, I also worked in tandem with the company's various programming, marketing, and promotional teams on maintaining a presence for the satellite radio giant at large-scale events, including Lollapalooza, Bonnaroo, SXSW, Coachella, Governor's Ball, The Rolling Loud Festival, The B.E.T. Awards/Experience Weekend, the Essence Music Festival, The Soul Train Awards, LL Cool J's Rock the Bells Festival, and The Soul Train Cruise, among others.

During my ten years at SiriusXM, I curated hands-on recorded content for artist-dedicated pop-up channels for Prince, Aretha Franklin, Whitney Houston, Notorious B.I.G., 2-Pac, and Miles Davis, as well as building channels honoring Janet Jackson, Alicia Keys, Motown, Tina Turner, and The Apollo Theatre. I was responsible for booking talent for the channels and programmers that I worked with, including LL Cool J's Rock the Bells Radio, Heart & Soul, Bob Marley's Tuff Gong, The Groove, Soul Town, The Jimmy Jam Show, SiriusXM F.L.Y., Kirk Franklin's Praise, Silk 330, Real Jazz, Smooth Jazz, Urban View, Studio 54 Radio, and the All Music is Black Music podcast.

In my professional capacities, I've worked with veteran artists from New Edition to Boyz II Men to Earth, Wind & Fire, and Janet Jackson to A Tribe Called Quest and Run-D.M.C., as well as contemporary superstars and up-and-coming artists such as The Migos, Cardi B, Wiz Kalifah, NE-YO, Victor Manuelle, J. Balvin, Luis Fonsi, Bad Bunny, Andra Day, Post Malone, Chloe & Halle, A Boogie Wit Da Hoodie, H.E.R., Ella Mai, Khalid, Juice WRLD, and many others.

The most important lesson I've learned in this business is to find your passion. I'll repeat it, Find your passion, and you'll find your road to success. When you love what you do, it's no longer work; it's passion!

Tracey J. Jordan has been honored for her community-minded endeavors and has served as the Vice-President and currently serves on the Board of Governors for the N.Y. Chapter of the Recording Academy (the GRAMMYs). Jordan received the New York Urban League's Building Brick Award in 1988. The Environmental Media Award for the video "Mercy, Mercy Me (The Ecology)," in 2022, received the T.J. Martell Foundation's Women of Influence Award. In October 2023, she received the Mike Bernardo Female Executive of the Year Award from the Living Legends Foundation.

Find Your Passion

Tracey with Snoop Dog

Tracey with The Migos

Mic Check 17

"Breaking Records by Icons"
~by~
Vida Dyson-Nash

As a Woman Behind The Mic, celebrating 50 years of Hip-Hop music, there is definitely an energy of gratitude! Hip-Hop has been a journey of empowerment through the expression of music and the landscape to my life since 1980 starting with "Rapper's Delight."

Raised in a family of broadcasters (WGCI Radio - Chicago), I was introduced to broadcast media at the early age of 5 years old. Broadcasting set my soul on a musical journey of wanting to hear new music first on the radio in all genres. Radio was my passion that would set my life's journey on an epic ride into R&B and Hip-Hop music. I remember over hearing "Rapper's Delight" and "The Real Roxanne" in a DJ radio programming meeting for the first time, wondering if radio would embrace this new sound of music that hadn't been yet defined in media. I knew at that moment, I had to be a part of this new exciting sound and culture!

There are so many memorable moments in Hip-Hop that I want to reflect on. One of my earliest memories is meeting one of the best lyricists ever: "Guru" of Gang Starr!

Wanting to submerse further into Black culture, I attended Clark University in Atlanta, Georgia, for two years beginning in 1981, majoring in Communication Media Arts. During my tenure there, I had the privilege of meeting one of Boston's finest, Keith Elam, better

Photo Credit: Uplife LLC

known as "Guru" of the duo Gang Starr. Keith's energy and drive was so heightened and filled with star power even back then, I felt he was destined for greatness. We used to share our dreams of him becoming iconic in Hip-Hop culture and me in music and broadcasting. It was pretty powerful to see those early thoughts of Hip-Hop musical ideas become real and manifest into a lifestyle that we could only dream about back in the Morehouse Dorms, and witness it come full circle.

I remember running into Guru at a BET Hip-Hop Awards where we embraced and caught up on Hip-Hop music and life in general, then promised to stay in touch. However, that was the last time I would see him. He passed away in 2010 at The Good Samaritan Hospital in Suffern, New York, which was actually the township where I lived at the time. I never knew he was sick as he kept it very private. I wish I had known as he was so close to my home. I would have visited him surely if I had known those would be his last days.

In 1990, I received the opportunity to work at RCA/Jive Records as Northeast Promotion Marketing Director. Jive was then the home of Grammy-winning rap duo Jazzy Jeff & the Fresh Prince. Barry Weiss, the Owner/CEO, Tom Carrabba, who was SVP of Marketing, and Roland Edison, VP of Promotion Marketing of Jive Records were excited for the "Summertime" single release slated for Summer 1991. At first listen, I knew it had the potential to become a radio smash and was excited to break this single in the Northeast territories at radio and retail stores. Philadelphia was the first market to support the single with airplay at WUSL, being that this was the hometown of Will Smith and Jeff Townes.

Jive asked the marketing staff to create a Radio/College promo tour. I remember dedicating countless hours of driving to retail and radio stations with music singles, vinyl and P.O.P. (point of purchase) merchandising for meet-and-greets promoting the "Summertime" single. DJ Jazzy Jeff & The Fresh Prince had released singles as early as 1988 but didn't have big success at mainstream radio until July of 1991 with "Summertime." This was the lead single from their fourth studio album, *Homebase*. It spent 18 weeks on the *Billboard* Hot 100 Chart, peaking at Number 4 and at Number 1 on *Radio & Records* Hot R&B and Hip-Hop Chart. Will and Jeff then won a Grammy for Best Rap Performance by a Duo in 1992 for that track.

As a marketing rep, I witnessed the evolution of Will Smith in Hip-Hop culture at Jive Records with "Summertime" and again at Columbia Records with his solo album *Willennium* in 2001. His determination and spirited personality have never wavered in his commitment to Hip-Hop and film. Like Guru of Gang Starr, Will gave that same star power; he believed and hoped that he would be one of the greatest to ever do it in music and film and I believe he has proven himself with his life's work.

It definitely was a team effort in delivering a *Billboard* Top Five Single and *R&R* Hip-Hop Number 1 on "Summertime," but it felt more like a boys' club celebration rather than a team-effort celebration. Back in the late '80s early '90s, women weren't getting the respect in Hip-Hop Music that they do today.

Breaking hit records at radio and being a part of the development of iconic artists while watching the evolution of Black culture evolve in music, fashion, and pop culture was – in a word – priceless. In addition to Will Smith & DJ Jazzy Jeff ("Summertime"), I helped break records by Too Short ("The Ghetto"), Kool Moe Dee ("Knowledge Is King") Queen Latifah ("U.N.I.T.Y."), Naughty By Nature ("Roll With The Flava"), Nas ("Stillmatic"), Lil Bow Wow ("Bow Wow" featuring Snoop Dogg), and other singles at radio.

As I reflect on the women executives in the music industry, we weren't always heard or taken seriously but once heard we always showed up and showed out! Hip-Hop culture had to embraced women in Hip-Hop and the brilliance we brought to this musical art form.

For me, observing and working with women in Hip-Hop was a whole new energy of empowerment. In 1993 I had the honor of working at the iconic Motown Records label which released Queen Latifah's album *Black Reign* via Flavor Unit. That was when I was introduced to "U.N.I.T.Y" Dana Owens, or, as the world knows her, "The Queen" aka Queen Latifah! On my first listen, I set my goal on making it the anthem of the Northeast territory for women. Meeting Queen Latifah and her mother, Rita Owens, was life changing as it was refreshing to see a mother/daughter team that was authentic, empowering and about the business of music with meaning in Hip-Hop.

When the going gets tough, the tough women get going! An impressionable moment for me with Dana aka Queen Latifah and her mother was at a 1993 radio event at WUSL-FM Philadelphia's Women's Empowerment Concert. The station asked for Queen Latifah to headline the concert event at last minute. Can I just say that whatever could go wrong, did go wrong with sound check, transportation arriving on time, and inclement weather, as it was an outdoor event. But let me just tell you, when my nerves were on 10, Ms. Rita kept everyone calm and on point! She was so calm, loving, and wise, and coached us all in a lesson of determination, follow-through, and finishing strong! The "Queen's" dynamic energy and charisma rocked the house and Latifah and I were forever Sheroes to the Program and Music Directors of WUSL-FM.

I too have had the privilege of observing and living upfront with two of my colleagues and sisters in the music industry: Sylvia Rhone, currently CEO of Epic Records, and Cynthia Johnson, currently V.P. of Promotion Marketing, Epic Records. I've watched Sylvia break iconic artists such as MC Lyte, Missy Elliott, Busta Rhymes, and Rah Digga at Elektra Records via my amazing husband, veteran promotion exec Richard Nash, and Cynthia "CJ" Johnson break The Fugees, Wyclef Jean, Lauryn Hill, Nas, Bow Wow, Wil Smith, and Jermaine Dupie at Columbia Records. Those years were epic and filled with Number One hit records.

It always amazed me to see in Hip-Hop culture how very different it was to break the men as Hip-Hop artists from the women. Most notable was the style and appearance of the artists. The men would come styled rugged, swaggy with Timberlands, baseball cap, hoodie, baggy jeans – and even sometimes worn sloppy. Whereas the women were supposed to compete with that same street swag and still be fit, presenting a certain body frame and style of clothing for their imaging.

Queen Latifah and Missy Elliott set the stage for originality in music and fashion and were among the first to define couture Hip-Hop fashion. I'll never forget the artwork for "U.N.I.T.Y.": The "Queen" wore a kufi which had never been worn before by a female artist, as in Africa it's known to be worn by kings. I believe Kool Moe Dee also wore a kufi in most of his single and album artwork. He always wore a kufi when we visited radio as it was always a topic of discussion. Teaching and expressing Black culture was very important to Queen Latifah and Kool Moe Dee, as conscious rap was very much the message in the early '90s Hip-Hop culture.

Another memorable moment is when Missy "Misdemeanor" Elliott wanted to shoot her "The Rain (Supa Dupa Fly)" video in black plastic garbage bags. I remember Richard telling me how in the marketing meeting all the executives were in an uproar and adamant in wanting to control Missy's wardrobe, as she was a little heavy back in the day. Missy wanted the world to focus on her art of music and not her weight. The label was very mindful of the fact that Missy was unique and refreshingly original with her music and in all of her videos, as back then it was considered weird and different! With today's artists, "weird and different" is considered to be super dope, swaggy and fashionable.

Today, the spirit of Hip-Hop culture is ingrained in my family and me! It's a part of our DNA, if you will. My son listens to pretty much everything Hip-Hop. His first Hip-Hop concert was a Hot 97 Summer Jam which forever changed his life! Drake and Kendrick Lamar are his favorites, and to see his face at that concert was an epic thrill for certain. I'm not sure who I'd be without witnessing those moments in time where Hip-Hop music evolved into this beautiful array of music, fashion, and art that it has become in 2023 with digital streams and NFTs. However, I'm super grateful for this life we call Hip-Hop and the journey it has taken me on.

In the words of Naughty By Nature, "hip-hop hooray ho hey ho hey ho hey ho hip-hop hooray"!

Vida Dyson-Nash

Vida Dyson-Nash is founder/CEO of UpLife LLC. She is a recipient of Cambridge's "Who's Who for Entertainment Excellence" and continues to mentor and consult industry visionaries. . and continues to be a forerunner in the music industry. Vida is a resident of Las Vegas and is the proud mother of a son who is a professional race car driver with International Motor Sports Association.

Stephen Hill, Vida, Will Smith "The Fresh Prince"
Photo Credit: Stephen Hill

Vida with her Platinum "Summertime" Plaque, and a Queen Latifah Black Reign CD
Photo Credit: Tuesday Conner

Mic Check 18

"Rakim: The God of Rap"
~by~
Jacqueline Rhinehart

In 1997 I was the first marketing head of a new record company that eventually became Universal Music. Also in 1997, New York rap artist Rakim was on the verge of his latest album release, *The 18th Letter: The Book of Life*. This was technically his first album without former partner Eric B.

I didn't know he was referred to as "The God" of rap, but I did know he'd been crucial to my fitness routine for years—his music—transforming my power walk from a "need-to-do" into an "I-gotta-do." His lyrics, topics, rhymes, and rhythmic cadence were the motivation that willed my morning discipline and presence of mind.

I evolved listening to Rakim. As the song goes, "there's levels to your love." Rakim was another level.

So when his project hit my desk at Universal Records—not only was I prepared to fight for his current project, but his catalogue, too! That was the ground I stood on when I addressed Jean Riggins, President of Black Music, and Doug Morris, the label's co-founder and chairman, about the proper album configuration: A double CD—his new set with his previous project. His new release, his "reintroduction," had to be a double CD—new tracks coupled with his vintage masterpieces. RAKIM in Toto! In other words, "'allow me to reintroduce myself'" should be the theme for all aspects of the project.

And we did just that, in a nutshell:
- Artwork by acclaimed abstract painter/arts photographer Adger Cowans and art directed by renowned abstract painter Danny Simmons with liner and album artwork gallery portraits curated by Danny Simmons.
- A major album listening party event at the SoHo Art Gallery, where massive canvasses of the original liner art was displayed.
- Poetry readings /dramatic recitations were performed by Sonia Sanchez, Prof. Michael Eric Dyson, Busta Rhymes, Treach, and twelve additional rappers performed at New York's Joseph Papp Public Theater and videotaped for broadcast. It was produced by MTV's Penny Mack.
- Publicized on Magic Johnson's late night talk show where Rakim and panel guests Michael Eric Dyson and Sonia Sanchez chopped it up with Magic Johnson, before *Dancing with the Stars* and *American Idol*) and his band.
- Performances backed by the renowned Ray Chew (current Music Director for TV hits A massive outdoor display campaign in 22 designated marketing areas (DMAs), including a New York City billboard campaign sponsored by urban clothing brand Marithè Francois Girbaud as well as in major cities.

The supporting marketing was deep and prolonged, including 500,000 direct mail pieces (not digital, but actual four-color fliers printed and delivered to physical mailboxes!) in top DMAs and a national radio and TV advertising campaign. This second campaign also included billboards in New York City sponsored by Marithè Francois Girbaud.

Our campaign was an intense and prolonged attack. We achieved gold and platinum status, gratified that we could help a project that was worthy. We gave as good as we received.

All hail the god of rap: RAKIM.

Rakim: The God of Rap

Jacqueline "Jackie" Rhinehart is an executive who has reached the pinnacle of success in two important areas of the music industry, Marketing and Publicity. As the first Sr. Vice-President of Marketing at Universal Records, (Universal Music Group), which encompasses the legendary Motown Records, she directed multi-million-dollar advertising and media campaigns, as well as developed successful cross-promotional ventures among Universal/Motown artists with blue-chip companies such as Coca-Cola, Seagram's, Budweiser and Viacom- owned BET and MTV among others. Artists like Nelly, Erykah Badu, Cash Money, Boyz II Men, and Sean "P-Diddy" Comb's highly successful Bad Boy Entertainment have all benefited from this brilliant and "go get 'em" executive.

Prior to her long tenure at Universal, she served as Sr. Director of Publicity at Arista Records under the leadership of legendary music impresario Clive Davis. Overseeing the Urban Publicity Department, she developed campaigns for a wide variety of artists that included Dionne Warwick, Whitney Houston, Toni Braxton, TLC, Lisa Stansfield, Kenny G. and the Queen of Soul Aretha Franklin. During her tenure at Mercury Records, it was Ms. Rhinehart who helped transform a former Miss America, Vanessa Williams, into a gold and platinum-selling artist. Jacqueline currently grows organic food on the 27-acre farm where she resides in South Carolina.

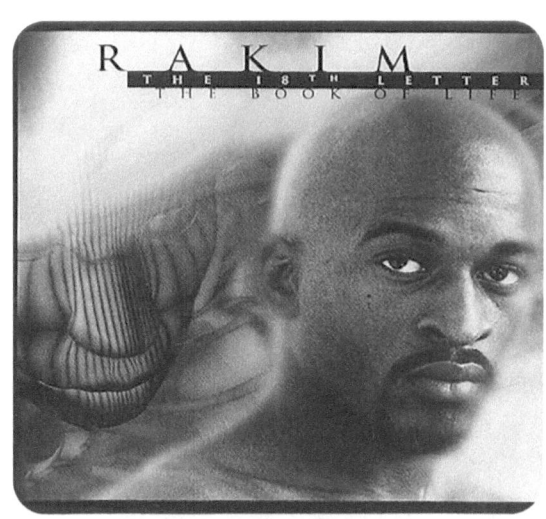

Rakim album cover

Mic Check 19

"Erasure? Send My Flowers Please"
~by~
Tami Cobbs

My love for music started as a child in Red Bank, New Jersey. My parents and older brother, Tyrone, were music aficionados who constantly played music that captured my imagination and made me feel like I was right in the middle of a live performance.

Tyrone was a devoted music enthusiast, introducing us to artists like Jimi Hendrix, Gil Scott-Heron, and Earth Wind and Fire. I was captivated by the incredible sounds he created with his extensive and expensive music equipment.

I discovered my love for Hip-Hop from the first moment I heard "Rapper's Delight" by The Sugarhill Gang. I can vividly recall the iconic blue album cover that sparked my lifelong love for this dynamic and influential art form.

Since the age of 3, I participated in various activities such as tennis, horseback riding, swimming, ice skating, and gymnastics. When my parents suggested I choose one activity to focus on, I honed in on gymnastics as I was naturally drawn to the trampoline.

My passion for trampoline motivated me to train harder, resulting in world travel for competitions. Through hard work and dedication, I won the 15-17 World Age Group Championship Games in Osaka, Japan, in 1984. This was such a pivotal moment in my trampoline career because my dad was hospitalized at the time, and it didn't look good. Honestly, I was afraid to go because I wasn't sure he would be there when I returned home. I was so proud to have returned home as a champion for my Daddy—he was one of my greatest inspirations.

I continued to excel and won the Women's National Trampoline Championship in 1985 and 1986. To further my skills, my mom supported my decision to move to Lafayette, Louisiana, and train under the guidance of renowned coach Leigh Hennessey during my junior year of high school. Despite being away from home, I was determined to pursue my dreams. I returned home mid-year to graduate with my senior class and held onto my Women's National Trampoline title in 1987. My ultimate dream was to compete in the Olympics. However, Trampoline was not an Olympic sport at the time.

In the summer of 1988, my sister Lashawn and I decided to attend a Tony, Toni, Toné, concert in Long Island, New York. On our way in, we met Diana Finley and Ta-ning Conner, who had backstage access. Diana worked in the music industry; Ta-ning was a model. I joined them backstage and was thrilled to meet my favorite performers. Later that night, Diana mentioned that I had the personality for public relations and proposed a potential opportunity to work in the music industry.

While I had always considered a career in the music industry, I didn't know how to pursue it. Now, I was overjoyed to have a new friend who could point me in the right direction. Plus, she lived in NYC. At the time, I was living on the Jersey Shore. At that moment, I realized I needed to start planning and exploring my options further. I hastily reached out to Diana the very next day and arranged to meet up a few days later. Little did I know that this decision would lead me on a path toward success.

My new friend, Diana, introduced me to Jane Blumenfeld, who was head of a company called In-Media Publicity. Following my interview with Jane, it became clear that this was a match made in heaven. Under her tutelage, I had the opportunity to work on her most coveted account, *The College Media Journal/CMJ*. Jane had a bigger-than-life personality. Working alongside her, I honed my skills in marketing and advertising, as well as the art of effectively pitching ideas to journalists and capturing media attention. I was responsible for accompanying artists to and from various press events. It was my first time working closely with Hip-Hop artists and engaging with the press.

Some notable names I had the pleasure of working with were WC and The Maad Circle, Coolio, Bobcat, LL Cool J, DJ Pooh, and Ice Cube.

This opportunity was especially significant as the CMJ Music Marathon conference at the former World Trade Center was my last event with In-Media Publicity before the company closed its doors. Jane asked me about my future goals and interests. I shared my passion for pursuing a career in public relations from the label side. With her support, I secured an internship at LaFace Records, based out of the Arista offices in New York City. Under the guidance of Lesley Pitts, the director of publicity for LaFace, I learned valuable PR skills and techniques. Lesley's training left a lasting impact on me as I strived to emulate her exceptional skills. Audrey LaCatis, from Arista, was also a great mentor.

During my stint at Arista, I met mega-producers/songwriters Babyface and L.A. Reid, the founders of LaFace Records. This opened my eyes to the immense opportunities within the music industry. My passion intensified when I got involved in the *Boomerang* soundtrack project and gained firsthand experience in label PR and music conferences.

Chung King Recording Studios

My days started at Arista and ended at the former Chung King Recording Studios (CKRS) in lower Manhattan. I had the opportunity to work with Hip-Hop group Leaders of the New School during the recording of their 1991 debut album *A Future Without A Past*. During my time at CKRS, I gained a wealth of knowledge about budgeting and album credits in the recording industry. This experience proved indispensable in my later role as a music manager.

The stars were aligned just right. Diana was now working with Francesca Spero, the head of publishing at Def Jam. Diana told me about a rising group called Mobb Deep, who were always hanging around Def Jam. They called her looking for artist management. She asked me if I was interested. Of course! I jumped on this opportunity, and I was eager to take on my first management challenge.

Erasure 1: No Credit, FlipMode/Rowdy Records

When Dallas Austin's label, Rowdy Records, joined the Arista Group in 1992, I was determined to forge a business relationship with him and his brother Claude. However, I was uncertain about how to make this happen.

With my deeper grasp of the music industry, particularly in the realm of public relations, I was certain I could make something happen. Building a positive reputation and expertly showcasing my ability to bring people together involved a potent blend of self-assurance, effective communication, and perfect timing.

Luckily, my good friend and mentor at the time, Donald Francois, was working with Busta Rhymes from Leaders of The New School. He mentioned that Busta was interested in launching his own label. This sparked an idea for me. I cautiously broached the topic with Dallas and Claude, proposing the idea of giving Busta a label deal on Rowdy Records. It was a gamble, but one that ultimately paid off.

With a surge of excitement coursing through me, I eagerly took on the challenge of orchestrating the logistics necessary to fully broker the deal, bringing the Flip Mode Squad to Rowdy Records. It was a groundbreaking opportunity for Rowdy, and after numerous productive meetings, we reached a successful agreement. This moment marked the official birth of FlipMode/Rowdy Records, a feat that would not have been possible without my vision. I was never acknowledged for my efforts, not one time, hence, my first experience with "erasure." I didn't fully understand that for women, this was our "normal." I couldn't help but savor the thrill of this new accomplishment, even as I juggled my early work with Mobb Deep and my recent departure from Arista.

Erasure 2: No Album (EP) Credit, Mobb Deep

My most significant Hip-Hop contribution: Creating and cultivating the environment for one of the all-time greatest Hip-Hop albums in history—Mobb Deep's 1995 album *The Infamous*—and sparking the environment for Havoc to become one of the greatest Hip-Hop producers of all time.

When I met Mobb Deep's Havoc and Prodigy, I realized they were young men. My business partner and childhood friend, Sandra " Peachie" Bynum, and I decided to first meet their parents and let them know about our involvement in their careers. The meetings proved to be a success and Managing Artist Careers (MAC) Management was born.

Peachie and I had a vision of forming an all women-run, women-owned management company that would be the equivalent of Rush Management. We had the flyest, most outstanding logo: It was a Nefertiti whose afro had the letters MAC carved in it. In preparation, we read lots of books, among them *Billboard*'s "Guide to Successful Artist Management" and *All You Need to Know About the Music Business* by Donald Passman, and others wanting to be the best new artist management company with a women's touch.

Collaborating with Mobb Deep was an extraordinary experience. Becoming acquainted with them felt like bringing two younger brothers into my family, and in some ways, like gaining two adopted sons. In July 1991, their demo caught the attention of *The Source* Magazine's "Unsigned Hype" column, ultimately leading to their record deal with 4th & B'way/Island Records.

As their manager, I was introduced to some of the label's Black music staff and artists, to name a few: Kelly Lynn Jackson, Kedar Massenburg, Daddy O, and Al "Butter" McLean. However, in our first meeting, it became clear that the group needed to part ways with this label, and I was left to ponder, "How can I fix this situation?" The previous managers had embezzled the recording budget, leaving no funds for the group's album to be worked. As I sat through endless meetings at 4th & B'way, I could feel the energy in the group slowly dissipating. The lack of interest and depleted budget made it clear that it was time for a change.

Juvenile Hell, the debut album that dropped on April 13, 1993, had two workable singles: "Peer Pressure" and "Hit It from the Back," which solidified the duo's status as rising stars in Hip-Hop. As I searched for a new recording deal, my primary goal was to showcase the group's talent through live performances of our top single, "Peer Pressure." Then I learned that BET's popular Saturday show "Teen Summit" was seeking meaningful entertainment centered around the topic of peer pressure. I immediately reached out to my good friend Brian Harris, the show's esteemed lighting designer, to explore the possibility of Mobb Deep performing. Through my persistence and persuasion, I secured an extra budget from the label for our group's first on-air television performance. The result? A smashing success, solidifying Mobb Deep's spot as a dominant force in the industry. It was our last full-blown collaboration with 4th & B'way/Island Records.

Meeting after meeting to determine our next steps at 4th & B'way and after several attempts at good faith negotiations I was able to secure the release of the group. In a moment of determination, I reached out directly to Steve Rifkin at LOUD Records in 1994. At first, it seemed like a long shot. Matty C, a former writer for *The Source*-turned-A&R rookie, saw potential in our duo. With Steve's offer of a $60K budget, our dream became a reality and LOUD Records became our new home.

My top priority was hiring a business manager. After the unfortunate incident at 4th & B'way, it became clear that my group needed proper education on financial management and access to their own financial records. I also hired a separate attorney to represent the group's interests. As the manager, I took on a role that was often daunting but always rewarding. I dedicated myself to ensuring the success of the group. I worked tirelessly as if I were part of the label staff.

I represented all things creative for Havoc and Prodigy. I collaborated with the RCA art department, carefully considering, and ultimately rejecting, any photos featuring guns on the album. I was the voice for all final business decisions on their behalf. I sought outside expertise and consulted with marketing exec (and Women Behind The Mic co-founder) Michelle Joyce and Donald Francois to develop a marketing campaign as I was dissatisfied with the label's marketing plan. My request for a marketing budget was denied. Determined to represent my group in the best possible light, I took matters into my own hands and personally crafted the marketing plan.

My Chung King Recording Studio experience came into play. As I was closely managing our recording budget, I was also teaching the label's A&R rookies Matt Life, aka Matty C, and Schott "Free" Jacobs how to properly write album credits. I made sure to be present at all recording sessions to ensure the focus remained on creating quality work rather than indulging in distractions or leisurely activities. The "out of sight, out of mind" approach was not an option for me on this project. I made it a point to physically visit LOUD Records' office at least three times a week to ensure that everything was progressing smoothly.

We put in a lot of effort and long hours, but ultimately, we successfully delivered what would go on to become one of the greatest Hip-Hop albums of all time, *The Infamous*, all while sticking to our budget. As we settled into our new home at LOUD Records, little did we know it would quickly turn into a nightmare. The label brass took it upon themselves to make decisions for my artist, completely disregarding our management team. This included scheduling recording sessions with A Tribe Called Quest's Q-Tip and other producers, without consulting us and affecting our budget.

In retrospect, this can be categorized as "erasure": Being completely overlooked as if the two of us were invisible, only because we are women. We always worked in the spirit of partnership with the label to make the process seamless, but it became more and more apparent that the label didn't see us as their partner.

After causing us intense disappointment with their dismissive actions, the label also rejected our request for EP credit. I immediately arranged a meeting with the label to discuss the situation. In addition to myself and Peachie, our attorney, the group's attorney, and our business manager were also in attendance. I wanted the label to know that my team was strong, and that we had proper representation.

At the meeting, Steve asked Arty Erk, the business manager, what he was doing there. Arty responded, "I am the group's business manager." To my surprise, I found out later that Steve's dad, Jules Rifkin, was one of Arty's associates. Arty's presence at the meeting did have some impact. The respect level changed, but not by much. The legal documentation signed by Mobb Deep, giving Peachie and I rights to EP credit, didn't mean a thing. We were "erased" right in front of the eyes of the men who saw us grind, day after day after day.

Our hard work rewarded LOUD's A&R rookies, Matty C and Schott Free. They received EP credit and royalties from the initial debut of *The Infamous*. Royalties paid right to this very day of a project that has sold more than 1,100,000 copies, not including international sales. This experience has left a painful and lasting impact, even today.

To top it off, we were not even honored with a platinum plaque. It's clear that we were not even considered important enough. It still feels like the final straw on a long list of disappointments.

We continued to manage Mobb Deep for two years after that and provided mentorship and support through Prodigy's health issues related to sickle cell anemia.

With newfound fame and money, not to mention being young impressionable, with numerous voices vying for their attention, Mobb Deep eventually signed under the guidance of Violator chief Chris Lighty.

Meanwhile, during a promotional tour with the group, I encountered the presence of one of the most talented, beautiful souls on the planet, Ms. Erykah Badu in her hometown of Dallas, Texas. The meeting led to a new music industry chapter.

Erasure 3: No Discovery Credit, No Point, No Employment - Erykah Badu

Why is music executive Kedar Massenburg best known for bringing Erykah Badu to fame when I BROUGHT ERYKAH BADU TO FAME?? Let the women's choir say "AMEN!!!"

Mobb Deep and I were on the road doing promotional work in Texas. At a show in Dallas, their opening act was an artist by the name of Erykah Free. Currently known as Erykah Badu, Badulla Oblongata, Sara Bellum, Analogue Girl in a Digital World, and Manuela Maria Mexico, she blew us away with her opening act performance.

After the show, I immediately approached Erykah to inquire about artist management. To my disappointment, she informed me that she had representation. There was no one like Erykah, and her talent was raw. She was the complete package and I wanted to work with her. While she already had management, she did not have a recording deal and I knew just who to call.

Erykah gave me two demo tapes and put me in touch with her manager, Ward White. My plan was to call Kedar Massenberg. Kedar was responsible for D'Angelo's career, had coined the term "Neo Soul" and later trademarked it. My vision was to see Erykah as not only part of the neo-soul movement, but the Queen of Neo Soul, and I thought Kedar would be a good fit. Soon thereafter, Erykah became the first signed artist under Kedar Entertainment.

When I arrived home, I couldn't wait to share her press kit and demo cassette with Peachie and my roommate, Loyal Thomas. Peachie enjoyed it, but Loyal lost his mind as it was love at first listen. Erykah's demo tape became our daily radio play, so much so that we knew the lyrics to the entire demo within a matter of days.

I called Ward White to introduce myself and congratulate him on having such an amazing artist. We talked about our backgrounds and became familiar with each other's music industry history. He was open to the idea of me shopping the demo tape. Once he gave me the blessing, I was off to the races.

Full of excitement, I called Kedar and told him we needed to meet. I had a demo that was going to rock his world. Kedar was open. A few days later we met. I remember getting in his car to play the demo for him. He liked what he heard. He asked to hold onto one of the demo tapes and the press kit became his.

A few days later, I wasn't surprised when Kedar called me asking for her management contact. He told me he was going to offer her a deal. Erykah's manager, Ward, called to inform me that Kedar had put an offer on the table. Ward wanted to show his appreciation by offering a finder's fee for my work; Kedar also promised to match her offer, by giving me one point on the project and provide an opportunity for employment at Universal. At this point I was no longer working in a management capacity and had returned to college. Both Kedar and Ward are attorneys, so the deal happened without a hitch.

My roommate, Loyal, who was also part of my business team, played a big part in setting Erykah up for success at the grass-roots level. Her first New York City performance was at Malik Yoba's restaurant The Soul Cafe. The restaurant was sold out and the entire crowd knew the lyrics to Erykah's demo, which later became her first album, 1997's *Baduizm*.

Erykah's debut album sold 159,000 copies the first week of release, on its way to eventually selling 2.8 million copies. At the height of the Bad Boy era, *Baduizm* sold 3 million copies in the United States alone. I am certain copies are still being sold.

Erykah and I managed to stay in touch in the beginning stages of her project. I would check in on her and give her sisterly advice about the business from a woman's perspective. Her life was changing, quickly, as she amassed great levels of success. Erykah is the same, beautiful human today that I met more than 25 years ago, just more evolved. I appreciate her honoring her word and acknowledging me for believing in her right from the very start. It means so much.

I wish I could say the same thing about Kedar Massenberg, but unfortunately, it's the same old story of women in the music industry being made promises that men never honor. A classic case of "erasure.": No acknowledgement of discovery, no points, and no promise of work. I should mention that Kedar did throw me a third of what I was promised. I only received it because Erykah called him directly and I showed up, armed with a dominant male presence so I could leave with the pocket change he threw at me.

In closing, I'm reflecting on the questions this volume of *Women Behind The Mic* attempts to answer: What does it take for women to get their flowers? When will women get the overdue credit and acknowledgement for all the work we have done, the work we do and the work we will continue to do to ensure we are never "Erased"?

My final response: Ladies, take notes! Too often we have seen failure to secure the "bag" due to a lack of binding legal agreements and having our contributions ERASED. Whether this is due to inexperience or simply not being let in with a handshake, we have to make sure we know our value and our worth. We deserve a seat at the table, period!

I would like to acknowledge the men who do stand strong and tall, supporting their women and being their rock. Thank you, husband, for having my back in this male-dominant music industry and pushing me to be great. Life takes us in so many directions.

Today, Tami Cobbs is the Private Wellness Officer of Hands 2 Health 4 Us, utilizing the power of touch to impact the lives of others through restorative massage. She happily resides in New England with her husband and teenage son. She is a strong advocate for the differently abled community.

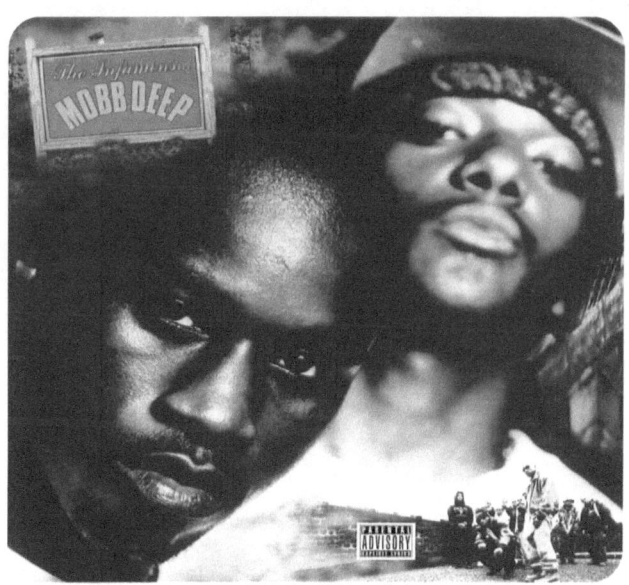

Mobb Deep album cover

Mic Check 20

"The Magnitude of Ms. Lauryn Hill"
~by~
Thembisa S. Mshaka

Author's note: I served humbly as the advertising and creative campaign writer for Ms. Lauryn Hill on her only two solo albums, The Miseducation of Lauryn Hill and MTV Unplugged 2.0. It is through this unique vantage point that I share my observations.

I met Lauryn Hill in 1994 in San Francisco. Tyesh Harris, Head of Rap Promotion at Columbia Records, made the introduction. They were in town for the *GAVIN* Seminar, held by the trade magazine for which I produced Hip-Hop panels and showcases as the magazine's first and only Black woman Rap Editor, before the conference began to travel to New Orleans, Atlanta, and San Diego. Upon meeting, L-Boogie and I instantly recognized self in one another: Two young Black women making their mark in Hip-Hop. Sometimes the journeyt felt like flying, more often than not, it felt like quicksand. We were both determined not to be swallowed up, and we chose to soar instead.

Lauryn's ascent may have felt mercurial, but she had been hard at work for years before her solo debut changed everything for women in all of music—not just rap. From her teenage days in Tranzlator Crew, to her role as a Fugee with Wyclef Jean and Pras Michel, Lauryn was laser focused on greatness because she had *come* from greatness.

Photo Credit: John Jay for Ashunta Sheriff Beauty

A loving, brilliant, and spiritually grounded family poured love and encouragement into her. A tight-knit Black community in East Orange, New Jersey, surrounded and nurtured her. Her own inner fire fueled her, and her talent, wide and deep in its range, fortified her.

No stranger to collaboration, she made magic as a contributor to the groups she inhabited. The Fugees became one of the most successful Hip-Hop groups in the history of the genre. *The Score*, it seemed, would never stop moving units. Cresting at 22 million sold worldwide, it is still the best-selling album of all time by any Hip-Hop group. It sold enough to take the Fugees' debut album *Blunted On Reality* triple platinum after a very quiet first week and never charting on the *Billboard* Top 200.

But no group dynamic could contain what Lauryn Hill possessed. Lauryn's artistic vision has always been laser-like, and what she had to say as a Black woman coming of age required *taking up* space, not sharing it with two other men. She never professed to have all the answers. But she knew what she knew. Her faith unshakeable, and her ability with pen and microphone undeniable, she embarked on the journey of miseducation as an idea—and intimate self-knowledge as the objective. This is a journey most Black women and girls take with neither fanfare nor magnifying glass, often left to unpack their missteps, pain and confusion with their innocence left as collateral damage. *The Miseducation of Lauryn Hill* would lay this journey bare. Raw with urgency and vulnerability, every song gave girls who looked like and felt like her permission to grieve, to forgive, and to heal.

The Miseducation of Lauryn Hill made it okay to be a young girl in progress. It also affirmed Black girlhood, in particular, in all its complexity and with no apology. And while Lauryn's impact as a public figure began with The Fugees—the gorgeous deep brown girl with that halo of an Afro, long braids for bangs, silver hoops alight in the dark movie theater of the "Killing Me Softly" video is unforgettable—it was cemented, canonized, actually, with her solo debut.

I had the distinct honor and privilege of being hired to write the advertising campaign for this album. It is why I was asked to come to

Sony Music as Senior Advertising Copywriter in June of 1998, just eight weeks before the album's August 25 release.

I had no formal advertising experience. It goes back to having already met Lauryn as a trade music journalist and knowing a helluva lot about Hip-Hop. While she was making her mark on the culture, I was parallel pathing, making mine. I had the good fortune to be in a national position from the West Coast, the Oakland/San Francisco Bay Area, to be specific. I had proven myself to be coachable under the editing tutelage and mentorship of Beverly Mire and Ben Fong-Torres (yes, *that* Ben Fong-Torres, the wordsmith whose journalism chops built *Rolling Stone*). I truly learned from the best. After five years running the *GAVIN* Rap charts and bestowing numerous covers (including the first career trade covers received by Common, The Lady of Rage, Scarface, Bone Thugs-N-Harmony, and D'Angelo) I got the job at Sony. Lauryn and I would cross paths again.

I knew I could do the job. I was excited about the prospect of having her steel sharpen mine. I knew that her having a young Black woman campaign writer would matter. In fact, I *set out to prove* to the label and to the industry that it would. I knew it would be the kind of hard work that I would love. What I didn't know was that this campaign would just keep going and growing for almost three years, causing my no-formal-advertising-training self to win the NARM (National Association of Record Merchandisers) Award for her "Most Likely To Succeed" double-page spread. We both knew that the album would be smash. The core team for the album's recording and marketing were on a mission to prove anyone who doubted this wrong. What we could never have predicted was the album being formative for the soul of a generation and ultimately, transformative for music itself.

The Miseducation of Lauryn Hill hit its 25-year milestone on August 25, 2023. Let's take a topline view of the magnitude of the album:

- The album sold 20 million units worldwide, with just three official singles

- Best-selling album by a female rap artist
- Best-selling debut week by any female artist prior to its release
- Record-setting first week sales among woman artists of all genres at 422,624 units
- Debuted at Number One on Billboard Top 200, making her the first solo woman emcee to top the all-format chart
- Garnered ten GRAMMY® nominations
- Won five GRAMMY® Awards, including the most coveted Album of the Year award
- First Hip-Hop album to win Album of the Year GRAMMY®
- Achieved RIAA Diamond Certification (10 million units sold in the U.S.)
- Ranked Number 10 on Rolling Stone's *500 Greatest Albums of All Time* list
- Placed Lauryn Hill on an unprecedented number of magazine covers for a woman rapper, including the covers of couture fashion magazines like *Harper's Bazaar* (September 1999) and hard news magazines like *TIME* (Feb. 8, 1999)

In 1999, The *Miseducation* Tour was sponsored by Levi's, which outfitted Hill and the band. This was a monumental partnership that no woman emcee had commanded until Lauryn Hill. This collaboration created the possibility of apparel brands partnering with Hip-Hop artists on a grand scale with mainstream visibility, affirming the fact that Hip-Hop is as American and popular as denim itself. Jamila Hubbard, Senior Manager, Diversity, Equity & Inclusion, at Levi Strauss & Co., had this to say on the company website about the album's impact on her life while she was in college: "… it was a big part of my development into being a woman, setting boundaries, loving myself, and having stronger self-esteem … it was one of those pivotal albums in your life." Mic drop.

With her inescapable, trailblazing media coverage engineered by Miguel Baguer, then Columbia Records VP of publicity and publicist for Lauryn Hill, and stunning, high-concept music videos commissioned by Camille Yorrick, then Columbia Senior Director of Video Production, Lauryn's media magnitude rippled like an earthquake, cracking open the beauty and fashion spaces previously reserved for porcelain complexions, wispy hair, and ethnically ambiguous women of color (on occasion). Dark skin, loc'd tresses, bangles, rings and necklaces inspired by the African diaspora. Natural fingernails, natural makeup to enhance her already otherworldly beauty and captivating smile.

Styled by Debra Ginyard for the album and with the Fugees before that, Lauryn became a fashion muse and a reference for all things cool, sleek, and effortlessly sensual, which only turned her into more of a sex symbol. People of all genders were crushing hard on Lauryn Hill. She unleashed a wave of trendsetting style, ranging from military streetwear and custom leather pieces to haute couture. She was just as fly in camo print as she was in a single string of diamonds; she wore it all like she belonged in everything she put on, despite opinions to the contrary, that sought to keep vocal Black girls in put places. Ms. Hill would never relent on her demand for the utmost respect.

This would hold true even as she refused to stay in the place to which she had ascended. Superstardom became a hostile work environment, and she spoke that truth to power with *MTV Unplugged 2.0*. Stripping production down to a bare acoustic essence, taking up guitar and trading long hair for a teeny weeny Afro, silk scarf, and baseball cap, her lyrics turned from a focus on love and relationships to liberation and rebellion.

In the moment, her audience, the industry...stunned. They recoiled, stung by a perceived betrayal, when Lauryn simply rejected an image she no longer wished to project. "I'mma be who I am ... it's freedom time," she sang on MTV. When her vulnerability wasn't in a "pretty" package, when it was motivated by her spirituality and not her naiveté, the media painted her as "emotionally unstable."

This narrative is convenient when a woman's truth doesn't depend on popularity, aesthetics, or external validation. And while the live album sold modestly compared to its predecessor, it was far from a sophomore slump, surpassing the RIAA certified platinum mark, garnering another GRAMMY® nod for "Mystery of Iniquity" (Best Female Rap Solo Performance), and debuting at Number Three on the Billboard Top 200. It has been hailed as one of the best live Hip-Hop albums ever recorded, and its lyrics proved to be prophetic in a pre-9/11 world. I like to remind her detractors and those with revisionist memories that even her "underperforming" album achieved enviable success on the charts and in sales.

And still, Lauryn Hill would not be contained. She exuded the light and fire of a star long before the world recognized her as such. Her ferocity as a lyricist, her anointing as a soul singer, remain unmatched in a single artistic human body. While she did not invent blending melody with rhyme within the genre, she certainly revolutionized it, giving Drake, Jah Rule, Missy Elliott, J. Cole, Nicki Minaj, and many others the green light to do their versions of what she'd done with "Killing Me Softly" and "Fugee-La." Lauryn Hill changed the sound of Hip-Hop forever. She made it possible for woman emcees—and indeed, women artists of all kinds—to be their whole, dynamic selves, with agency over their bodies and unwavering belief in their power.

On her feature with frequent collaborator Nas, from his album *King's Disease II* (2021), she rhymes "why would I join them when I know that I can beat 'em now? They put their words on me, but they can eat 'em now." Through controversy, peaks, and valleys, she continues to make sure we put maximum respect on her name.

That is the magnitude of Ms. Lauryn Hill.

Thembisa S. Mshaka is a 33-year veteran of the entertainment industry and the author of Put Your Dreams First, Handle Your [entertainment] Business. *A decorated creative and screenwriter, she has won numerous awards for creative excellence, including Clio and Gold Promax Global Excellence awards for her work in brand creative. On August 11, 2023, as Hip-Hop turned 50, Ms. Mshaka was inducted of the Bay Area Hip*

The Magnitude of Ms. Lauren Hill

Hop Archives for her contributions to Hip-Hop culture as a music trade journalist, campaign writer and media producer. It was The Miseducation of Lauryn Hill, *her very first creative campaign, that set her on course to becoming a world-class creative.*

Thembisa with Lauren Hill

Thembisa with Lauren Hill

Mic Check 21

"The Fairy Godmother"
~by~
Thomasina Perkins

I am known as a "quiet storm" who hails from the projects of Jersey City, New Jersey. The Booker T. Washington Projects to be exact.

I was lucky enough to be a kid who was very observant and wise beyond her years, as are most kids growing up in these environments, but I've always known I was "different." I was a lover of music at a very early age, and we were outside at a time when Hip-Hop was in its beginning stages. We weren't in NYC yet, just a Path train away. You couldn't go to the park, or to Journal Square, or even sit on the red benches outside our building without seeing the fashions, watching the b-boys break dance or the MCs battle or look up at a train and not see a graffiti artist's work go by. Even when my father joined the Army and moved us out of the projects, we stayed connected by family members and you guessed it … the music.

We didn't call it Hip-Hop then, we just knew that they rhymed, spit, kicked dope lyrics. As the new kids from "the north," we were the popular kids when we moved to Ft. Lewis, Tacoma, Washington, and we were crucial when we got stationed in Wurzburg, Germany, because between each duty station, we always went back home to Jersey and picked up the latest music, clothes, jewelry, etc. The summer we moved

Photo Credit: Hekima Qualls
Makeup & Hair: Axel Vasquez of Axel Makeup Academy

to Germany, "The Message" by Grandmaster Flash and the Furious Five was all the buzz in the States, but when we got to Germany, everyone there was still on "Rappers Delight" by Sugar Hill Gang, as the music and TV shows were months behind. So when you touched down from the States with the latest music, you were the IT, folks.

My cousins understood the assignment and kept us cool by sending us the latest music. Back then we were dubbing cassettes on a monthly basis, taping from stations like WBLS in New York, and Frank Ski or DJ Red Alert mix shows, etc., so we were always ahead. While in this space I fell in love with the music of Prince, Madonna, Whitney Houston, Michael Jackson and the Jacksons, The Cure, Def Leppard, Whitesnake, Kenny Rodgers, Dolly Parton, Reba McEntire, Pat Benatar, Pink Floyd, and the list goes on ... Did I say I was a lover of music?

Fast forward: Young adulthood, single mother to an amazing son, and working as a government civilian for the U.S. Navy and Department of Energy in the Nuclear Propulsion department, getting married to an Army Military Police officer, moving to Hawaii, giving birth to a beautiful daughter, coming back to the mainland and moving around; finally settling in the Washington, D.C., metro area as a divorced single mother of two, now a government contractor specifically working international programs and becoming a foreign military sales analyst (basically meaning I sold our government weapons systems to our "allied" partners) and, in between all of this, honing basic business, protocol, networking, and problem solving skills along the way.

One of my Admirals noticed I had a knack for people, places, and things, and thus my journey into public affairs began. The public affairs duties often sent me into the community, where I started meeting many creatives who– while incredibly talented –didn't have the business acumen of a flea. Well, common sense just wasn't so common, hence my being dubbed the #commonsensepr, as I couldn't understand how a nonprofit would hire an artist or athlete as a draw for a fundraiser, only to pay them more than what they raised. Can we say "counterproductive"?!

This led me to explore alternative ways of getting talent, finding the win/win in situations, and starting my "side hustle": Tru DIVA (Defining, Integrity, Vision, Authority) Productions, which in hindsight was a tad bit too female and too Black to be taken seriously, even though as a club party promoter it worked just fine.

During this time, I managed to land my first active star NFL player, Joshua Morgan a wide receiver for the then Washington Redskins (now Commanders), who had been traded from the San Francisco 49ers. I first met Morgan at one of the nightclubs where I was throwing parties with my daughter, as my wing woman, collecting our door money. By this time, I had become known around town as a friend to the creative community; being asked to listen in on up-and-coming artists at open mics; lending my business-side creative marketing tips to the likes of then-unknown Wale and Fat Trel; catching the eyes and ears of record executives, radio personalities and more athletes who wanted to be in the entertainment space, as sports and entertainment most certainly go hand and hand.

I was still not fully realizing that what I was doing was a skill that I could leave my government day job to pursue. Then one day I noticed that I was now also working with professional athletes Clinton Portis, Fred Smoot, Devin Thomas, and Vernon Davis; consulting with business owners and connecting them with mainstream artists; had joined the women's organization NABFEME (National Association of Black Female Executives in Music and Entertainment), led by former Def Jam executive Johnnie Walker, who I'm proud to say handpicked me to currently serve as the Network Director for the DC Metro area.

So I stopped telling God what he can't do, left my safety-net job, and established my firm, Capitol Public Relations, where I have worked with myriad of clients, including but not limited to CeCe Peniston, Lil Mo, Traci Braxton (God rest her soul), 4EY music group, and film production companies OCTET Productions and Be North Films, where I now boast about 19 titles as Unit Publicist and/or Locations Manager. I'm also business partners with Calvin "Snoop Dogg" Broadus with my "meet now" app Wink n Link, and with music and media mogul Russell Simmons.

This FINALLY brings me to why I called this chapter "The Godmother." I thought about some of my experiences throughout the years, evolving into an expert problem solver, reputation manager, and all-around crisis management professional. I originally thought I would call this chapter "The Clean Up Woman," but that implies that I'm just the help, and I'm so much more – in many ways, similar to the roles played by the late Clarence Avant, our dearly beloved, may he rest in eternal power. I am called upon not to simply clean up messes, I strategize how to prevent them in the future. I see things from a total standpoint, not just what's in front of us, blending all of my worlds together for the best possible outcomes while still holding my clients accountable.

For example, in the midst of Russell's legal storm, during the height of the COVID 19 crisis, our team pulled together an event to provide virtual aid for supplies utilizing Def Comedy Jam comedians for a night of relief and laughter. Hosted by Cedric the Entertainer, with music by Kid Capri, and directed and produced by Royale Watkins and Chris Spencer, the virtual event featured comics participating from their quarantined homes, including Mike Epps, Anthony Anderson, Michael Colyar, Bill Bellamy, Affion Crockettt, Spice Adams, Tiffany Haddish and others. We followed this with a special Def Poetry Jam hosted by the legendary Black Ice and Jessica Care, with such participating poets as Malcolm Jamal Warner and Newark Mayor Ras Baraka.

We threw our hats in political arenas – this is Hip-Hop grown up –with Dupre "Do It All" Kelley in Newark, where the Lords of the Underground rapper won his seat on the City Council the second time around and Def Jam comedian Rodney "Red" Grant, currently running as the Democratic Candidate for At-Large Member of the Washington, D.C., Council seat, helping him behind the scenes to navigate the nuances of moving from performer to politician with feet in both spaces concurrently.

Oftentimes being called at the last minute, I'd been dubbing myself "Last Minute Lucy." I used to question whether I should be flattered or insulted – insulted because I wasn't thought of first, then settled on flattered because they're now down to the wire and know I'll find a way to get it done, often with little to no budget. Not the most ideal space, and as I write this I myself need to re think this ...

My last example will be a little more specific. I was hired for a on- off issue by Interscope when top-selling artist Da Baby made misinformed and irresponsible statements about HIV. I worked with him and a group of representatives to have a conversation about why it was irresponsible and how to move forward. Now of course the initial reason was because he was losing ... I'll say invitations, and of course some wanted us to throw money at the issue, but that wouldn't solve the problem and this was a teachable moment. And in my world, that's what it's all about because, let's face it, the sun doesn't shine every day and someone has to know how to navigate in the eye of the storm. And, well, isn't that what a Godmother does? She stands in the gap, often thought to be unseen/unheard, but her impact is never unfelt. I tell all my clients, "I will ride with you through the bullshit, just don't bullshit me," and "You ain't got to listen, but you get your face cracked one too many times, my unconventional ways start to make sense."

In this business I've learned that my vast experiences and beautifully blended networks from government, corporate, non-profit, sports, music, TV, and film – basically all around entertainment – have equipped me with the tools and resources necessary to continually create common-sense, win/win outcomes. It's a wonderful thing when you don't concern yourself with who's name gets the credit because trust me, those that NEED to know absolutely know, so you don't have to be the flashiest one in the room or the most liked, but when you love what you do and believe in why you do it, they can't help but respect. And in my book, that's so much more than clean up, or simple help and PR strategy.

This is exactly the stuff Godmothers are made of.

Thomasina Perkins

Thomasina Perkins is the CEO and Principal Publicist at Capitol Public Relations which is a network of communication executives who provide reputational restoration, crisis management, public/media/community relations, and strategic brand consulting to corporate and individual clients. The mission is: To Operate in Boldness and Integrity, while helping Others Reach and Achieve their Dreams! She is currently the sitting president of the National Association of Black Female Executives. Thomasina is also a location scout and unit publicist for major motion pictures being filmed in the DC Metro area.

The fairy godmother hard at work making magic happen

Thomasina with Tiny and T.I.

Acknowledgments

A Love Letter to Hip-Hop
~by~
Michelle Joyce

Dear Hip-Hop,

As I reflect on my career journey, I'm flooded with memories: the highs, the lows, and the incredible path we've walked together. Entering EastWest Records as a young assistant, I had no idea that I was about to step into a world shaping my career, redefining my dreams, and becoming the soundtrack of my life.

You, my beloved Hip-Hop, have been the heartbeat of my career. From the start, you provided a platform to learn, grow, be mentored by boss women, and contribute significantly to music history. As I took my first steps, your beats echoed promises of moments that became milestones.

Plans evolve, and God's laughter reveals grander designs. Starting as an assistant, a mere apprentice in the grand orchestra of God's plans, being able to shatter that glass ceiling above me was sweet. A girl from the South Bronx, I never imagined being invited to CEO meetings for my expertise in Hip-Hop Marketing!

My biggest career moments unfolded in Hip-Hop—working behind the scenes at labels, founding an agency that launched Rocawear for Jay-Z—navigating a thrilling and challenging world with you as my constant, guiding me to unexpected highs.

The walls of my home are adorned with gold and platinum plaques—a testament to my victories. Each plaque tells a story of dedication, hard work, and those moments of magic when passion meets purpose. They are notes in Hip-Hop's symphony, echoes of personal triumphs.

Thank you, Hip-Hop, for resilience, passion, business, and life lessons. Your biggest gift: Allowing me to meet amazing women who are my chosen family, forever my people. Gratitude fills my reflection on our journey.

Hip-Hop, my blank canvas, has been painted with joy, and its beats forever fill my heart, shaping a career that brings immense happiness, strengthening my love for you over time.

Acknowledging the pivotal people who accompanied me on this journey:

- LJ: Sister for life, sister in Christ, your love and grace bring joy. God delivered you in response to my childhood prayer for a sister.
- Elissa Gabrielle: Sister and parent publisher, your unwavering support for the vision is truly appreciated. Thanks to your mom for guiding a young woman in the promotion side of the business.
- Contributors to the *Women Behind The Mic* Anthology Book Series: Your stories brought joy. We did that.
- Ma and Pa Kettle: Your love and support fill me with joy.
- Gini: My ride or die, forever.
- IW and Hezues: Brothers from another mother, thank you for believing in me and supporting my dream.
- Sistren: Thank you for standing with me in the best and worst times.
- Readers: Your interest and support are humbling.

Excited for what lies ahead.
Be Inspired. Always remember: You are magic.

Love, MJ

Acknowledgments

~by~
LaJoyce Brookshire

I am thankful to the Lord God Almighty for blessing me and this project beyond measure.

Michelle Joyce, Thank you for rocking with me for 30 years. I am thankful that the LJ/MJ Show is still in full swing. We've been rolling through ups, downs, over the rivers, and through the trenches together and we can't stop; won't stop now! LOL

Janine Coveney, Thank YOU for answering that call to take on the editing of this Edition. You are a Rockstar in the editing game. Also thank you for traveling to London with me to appear on behalf of this movement because you are the BEST roomie and dining partner ever!!

To all of the Sisters who said "YES" to this Edition, and submitted your stories by the deadline... I love you for standing with us in this endeavor. See you soon as we continue to tour the World.

To all of the Sisters from Volume One, Thank you for setting the stage for the Volumes to come and for appearing on stages from London to Las Vegas to share your stories.

Jessica Tilles, Thank you for seeing us and lending your lay-out talents to this body of work.

Elissa Gabrielle, Thank you for welcoming the Renewing Your Mind Ink family into the fold of Peace In The Storm Publishing.

Gus & Brooke Brookshire, Thank you for selling, promoting, and carrying boxes of books to events via planes, trains, and automobiles. Your support is the fuel in my tank to continue this work. Who Loves You?

To my Brothers IW, Chris, Hezues, Thank you all for doing what brothers do by holding me up and not being selfish in sharing your extraordinary talents with me and the world!

To Harry Lawson at Enigma Graphics, Thank you for another home run cover creation!

To Madyson Burton, Thank you for creating the hand drawing of the Women for this project! Your talent is extraordinary!

To everyone who purchased a book, coordinated a book signing event, referred us for a speaking engagement, extended Hospitaliaty, or wrote a review, I THANK YOU from the bottom of my heart.

WOMEN BEHIND THE MIC
"A Tribute"
~by~
LaJoyce Brookshire

Making deals Behind The Mic is her game,
And I bet, you don't even know her name,
...what a shame

Discovering and developing Stars for the stages,
Quietly earning those six figure wages.

She's in charge of the show and the flow,
and if you don't know, you'd never know!

She's the one in the room we need to mention,
Working that Black Girl Magic...So pay attention...

Classy, Sassy, Fabulous, and Fashiony.
Making moves Behind The Mic,
Working millions of Hits you know we like.

Sure, you can be a star and be done,
Question...have you got the skills it takes to make one?

They've built a strong and unique Sisterhood,
Planting them in record books as history should.

Their contributions to this music game have been significant,
For decades they've moved in stealth mode...like the Syndicate.

Now the Behind-The-Scenes stories are about to be told in Truthfulness,

Through Books. Documentaries. Lectures…It's Voluminous!

Asking yourself, "How Can I Be Down?",
Pay attention and stick around.

"Stay Ready, so you don't have to Get Ready",
Is the best advice EVER!
Get some education for success of any future endeavor.

The only way to attain a seat at this table,
Is to put in that work to prove you're able.

What is the acumen Behind The Mic plight?
Ask the Women - and it will be done right.

Who cranked out the work on the songs you know we like?
Now you know, it was the Women Behind The Mic.

Also Available in this Series:

Women Behind The Mic: Curators of Pop Culture ~ Volume One
"Word To The Wise"

Future Series Include:

Uptown Baby
The Bad Girls of Bad Boy
Aretha's Angels
The Wordsmiths
Purple Reign
All That Jazz
The Gospel Truth

www.ingramcontent.com/pod-product-compliance
Lightning Source LLC
Chambersburg PA
CBHW030523080526
44586CB00011B/301